Praise for MAKING ROUNDS WITH OSCAR

"Both touching and humorous. . . . It's about listening and letting go. It's also about the inner workings of a nursing home for Alzheimer's patients, the people who work there, the rhythm of their days, and the six other cats who also call it home, cats who also bring comfort to the dementia patients but do not share Oscar's talents of premonition."

—*USA Today*

"Beautifully written, heartwarming. . . . Told with profound insight and great respect for all involved, this is more than just a cat story (although it will appeal to fans of Vicki Myron's *Dewey*)."

—*Library Journal*

"Dr. Dosa's *Making Rounds with Oscar* lets us into his world and aims to inspire."

—*Parade*

"Dr. Dosa is a superb storyteller."

—Alzheimer's Association blog

"While Dr. Dosa portrays dementia and all of its difficulties, he provides hope and advice for caregivers who are coping with a loved one's decline. The book will inspire readers to discuss the critical but very difficult issue of end-of-life care."

—Delta Society blog

"At its heart, Dosa's search is more about how people cope with death than Oscar's purported ability to predict it. "

—Associated Press

"Dr. Dosa has written a book that compassionately addresses end-of-life issues. The stories he shares about residents and their families who must deal with such painful issues as Alzheimer's disease and other forms of dementia and terminal illness are tender and heartfelt."

—*Bibliophile by the Sea*

"A fascinating and humbling story."

—*Rhode Island Monthly*

"A touching story about Oscar the cat, his two-legged caretakers, and their patients."

—*Basil and Spice*

Making Rounds WITH OSCAR

Making Rounds WITH OSCAR

The Extraordinary Gift of an Ordinary Cat

David Dosa, M. D.

HYPERION
NEW YORK

 For information address Hyperion, 114 Fifth Avenue, New York, NY 10011.

Library of Congress Cataloging-in-Publication Data has been applied for.

ISBN 978-1-4013-2323-3
Paperback ISBN 978-1-4013-1043-1

Hyperion books are available for special promotions and premiums. For details contact the HarperCollins Special Markets Department in the New York office at 212-207-7528, fax 212-207-7222, or e-mail spsales@harpercollins.com.

Book design by Karen Minster

FIRST PAPERBACK EDITION

10 9 8 7 6 5

SUSTAINABLE FORESTRY INITIATIVE
Certified Fiber Sourcing
www.sfiprogram.org

THIS LABEL APPLIES TO TEXT STOCK

We try to produce the most beautiful books possible, and we are also extremely concerned about the impact of our manufacturing process on the forests of the world and the environment as a whole. Accordingly, we've made sure that all of the paper we use has been certified as coming from forests that are managed to ensure the protection of the people and wildlife dependent upon them.

Note to Reader

THE PATIENTS, THEIR STORIES, AND THE EXPERIENCES of caregivers confronting terminal dementia are based on my experiences caring for elderly patients. I am greatly indebted to the many people who shared their stories, including the staff at Steere House and the families of those who died with Oscar at their bedside. I truly believe that readers will be as moved by these accounts as I was when I first heard them and I have tried to remain as faithful to them as possible. I apologize for any factual errors that I have made in retelling the stories and in transcribing our interviews. If I have made errors, please know that they were unintentional.

Please note that for narrative purposes I have made some changes that depart from actual events. Moreover, in the interest of preserving confidentiality in patients with end-stage dementia, I have changed some names and modified some backgrounds to protect identities. Additionally, some of the characters that appear in this book are composites of multiple patients. Nevertheless, the experiences represented in this book are based on real-life patients and their caregivers whom I have been fortunate to care for over the years.

Finally, though I was skeptical early on, Oscar the cat's peculiar ability appears to be as real as it is mysterious, and he continues to regularly hold vigils over departing patients. It is my hope that readers will allow him to continue his "good work" unencumbered for as long as he chooses and will forgive the occasional mistakes that he makes from time to time. After all—no human (or cat) is perfect.

To the families and caregivers
of dementia patients everywhere

Making Rounds WITH OSCAR

CHAPTER ONE

"Animals are such agreeable friends—
they ask no questions, they pass no criticisms."

GEORGE ELIOT

IF YOU LOVE YOUR JOB, ON THE BEST DAYS YOUR WORKplace can seem beautiful, no matter how it might look to the rest of the world. An oilman looks at a flat, dusty plain and sees the potential for untapped fuel. A firefighter sees a burning building and runs into it, adrenaline surging, eager to be of use. A trucker's love affair is with the open road, the time alone with his thoughts—the journey *and* the destination.

I'm a geriatrician and I work on the third floor of the Steere House Nursing and Rehabilitation Center in downtown Providence. People tell me they would find my job depressing, but I'm always a little puzzled by that. Looking at my patients and their families, I have a remarkable view not just of lives well lived, but of deep commitment and love. I wouldn't trade that for the world. Sure, sometimes I'm caring for people at their worst, but I'm also blessed to be with them at their best.

My parents, both doctors, thought I was crazy for going into geriatrics. The family business has always been pediatrics—my mother and uncle are pediatricians, as was my grandfather. I think there was always this sense that I was choosing the wrong end of the life continuum to stake out my career. “Aren’t children so much cuter?” my mother would say.

I thought of going into pediatrics. I love children and babies, and have two little ones of my own. The difference for me has always been the stories. Children are a blank canvas, portraits waiting to be drawn. When we look at them, their lives just beginning, we feel a sense of renewal and an expanse of infinite possibility.

My older patients, on the other hand, are like rich paintings and boy, do they have stories to tell. On my best days I can look at them and see all the way back to their childhood. I think of their parents (long gone now), the places they’ve been, the things they’ve seen. To me it’s like looking through the other end of a telescope, back to the beginning.

That’s why Steere House looks beautiful to me—that and the fact that it’s a pretty nice place, as nursing homes go. The large, atrium-like windows flood each floor with light on sunny days, and on most days there’s music coming from the piano in the lobby. And then there’s Oscar. . . . I’d like to say I was the first one to notice his peculiar abilities—but I wasn’t. Thankfully there were others who were more astute.

THE UNIT had been empty that summer morning back in 2006, except for a pair of eyes that glared at me from atop the nurse’s desk. Like a warden cautiously evaluating a visitor to her facility, the questioning eyes sized me up to determine if I’d pose a risk.

“Hello, Maya. How are you?”

The pretty white cat made no move to greet me; she was consumed by the act of licking her front paws.

"Where is everyone, Maya?"

Aside from the cat, the third floor was strangely quiet. The hardwood-tiled corridors were vacant; the only signs of life were a few randomly placed walkers parked next to patients' doors. Empty now, these four-sided walkers seemed strange and unwieldy, like an imaginative child's Tinkertoy creation abandoned after play. At the far end of the east corridor, the morning light shone through the large picture windows, illuminating a broad swatch of the hallway.

I was looking for Mary Miranda, the day shift nurse. Mary is the source of all knowledge on the unit, a central intelligence agent who knows not just the story of every patient, but of Steere House itself. Though she's not technically in charge, there's little doubt among the physicians and staff as to who actually runs the floor. Mary is the maternal figure for each resident and she is fiercely protective of her children. Nothing happens on the unit without her knowing about it. Even her supervisors have been known to defer to her.

The doors to the residents' rooms are generally closed this early in the morning, and room 322, where Mary was performing AM care on her patient, was no exception.

I knocked on the door and heard a muffled voice telling me to hold on. As I waited in the hallway, I studied the corkboard display of family pictures attached to the wall outside Brenda Smith's room.

Mrs. Smith's full name, GERTRUDE BRENDA SMITH, and her date of birth, JANUARY 21, 1918, were stenciled in block letters on a rectangular piece of paper at the top of the corkboard. Each letter had been cut from construction paper and meticulously decorated with beads and other trinkets, the loving effort of some grandchild no doubt. Underneath the artwork there was a black-and-white photograph of a beautiful young woman in her early twenties. She wore dark lipstick that contrasted with her pale face, and she was fashionably dressed in a 1940s summer outfit. She was walking arm-in-arm with a handsome man in a Navy uniform. A parasol hung on her other arm. I imagined them in a park on a warm summer's afternoon shortly after the war. I studied their faces. They were happy, and clearly in love.

Beneath that picture was a second photograph of the same couple years later with two young children. This one was in color, the faded stock of an earlier day. His hair had receded some and hers now revealed a few streaks of gray. This picture contained a promise of a different sort. They weren't just young lovers now; they were proud parents, thinking of a future larger than their own.

The last picture in the collection was of Mrs. Smith in her later years, meticulously dressed, her silver hair neatly pulled back below a tastefully chosen hat. Her husband was gone, but she was surrounded by several generations. A banner hung in the background proclaimed HAPPY 80TH BIRTHDAY, GRANDMA. Eight years had passed since then.

I knocked again and made my way inside where Mary was tending to her patient. Gone was the vibrant, well-dressed grandma of the birthday picture. In her place was a smaller replica of the woman that was. Until I worked with patients in the late stages of Alzheimer's the expression "a shadow of her former self" was just a cliché. This is what I saw with Mrs. Smith and so many of the other residents here. But behind that shadow I still saw the substance, even if she seemed no longer to see me.

"Do you need me?" Mary asked, a little annoyed by the intrusion.

"Yes," I replied. "I need to know who has to be seen today."

"Let me finish up here and I'll meet you at the front desk."

As I turned to leave, Mary stood up from her stooped position at the bedside, arching her back against the strain.

"On second thought, David, I'm going to be busy here for a little bit. Why don't you go take a look at Saul's leg? It's red and angry looking. I think he has that skin infection again."

"Fair enough. I'll go see him."

I left the room and headed off in search of Saul Strahan, an eighty-year-old man who has lived on the unit for many years. I found him dressed in his usual garb—a Boston Red Sox sweatshirt and baseball cap—in his usual place, a La-Z-Boy recliner in front of the TV. The television was tuned to a morning talk show.

"What's on TV?" I asked, not expecting a reply.

I sat down beside him and glanced at the television. A young actress was telling the show's host how annoyed she was by the paparazzi that followed her everywhere.

"Everyone's got problems, right, Saul?"

I looked at him more closely. In addition to his progressive Alzheimer's, Saul had been the victim of a nasty stroke that had robbed him of his language four years ago. His eyes stared back at me with life, though, and I could sense that he was trying to speak. I placed my hand on his shoulder and told him that I was there to examine his leg.

As Mary had said, Saul's legs were both swollen with edema, a result of his twenty-year battle with congestive heart failure. Yet his right leg seemed angrier and decidedly warm to the touch. Mary's concerns seemed justified.

"Saul, my friend, I'm sorry but it looks like you're going back on antibiotics." I made a mental note to call his daughter.

I returned to the nurse's station where Maya remained hard at work cleaning her fur. Startled by my return, she leaped off the countertop, but not before giving me one of her *this place isn't big enough for both of us* looks.

I finished my note and sat at the desk waiting for Mary to return. A nurse for most of her life, Mary started as a nurse's assistant when she was in high school in the seventies and in nursing school discovered she loved working with old people. Not only is she one of the most dedicated nurses I know, she has some sort of intuition for the profession. She always seems to know who actually needs the most attention.

"Hello, sorry to keep you waiting." Mary's pleasant voice kept me from feeling too bad about my dependence. If she had been annoyed before it was all forgotten now.

"David, do you have a few minutes? I want to show you something down in room 310."

As we walked down the hall, Mary told me a little about Lilia Davis. "She's one of your colleague's patients. She's about eighty now, and has been here on the unit for eighteen months. About three months ago, she started losing a bunch of weight. Then one morning, she started to bleed from below.

We sent her to the hospital and they diagnosed her with colon cancer that had spread everywhere. Given her severe dementia, her family decided not to treat it; they sent her back on hospice services."

A reasonable approach, I thought to myself.

We found Mrs. Davis lying on her back, her eyes closed and her breathing shallow. A morphine pump was connected to her left arm via an IV. On the other side of the room was an empty cot, the sheets displaced off to the side. Someone had been sleeping here not long ago.

"Mrs. Davis's daughter," Mary said before I could ask. "I sent her home for a few hours to shower and change her clothes. I think she'd been here for thirty-six hours straight."

"So, what did you want to show me?" I asked.

Mary pointed to the base of the bed. "Take a look."

As I approached, the head of a black-and-white tabby cat rose up off the sheets. Moving caused the bell on his collar to jingle slightly. The cat's ears perked up and he glanced at me with questioning eyes. I ignored him and moved toward the patient. The cat put his head back down on his front paws and purred softly while nestled against Mrs. Davis's right leg. I looked over at her face and noted that she was clearly comfortable.

"She looks okay," I said. "Do you need an order for medication or something?"

"Not the patient, David. She's fine. It's the cat."

"The *cat*? You brought me in here to see a cat?"

"This is Oscar," she said, as if introducing me to someone at a dinner party.

"Okay," I said. I was starting to share Maya's bad mood. "He's a cat hanging out with a patient."

"Well, that's just it. Oscar doesn't really like to hang out with people. I mean, how many times have you actually seen him up here? Usually he's hiding somewhere."

It was true: I'd only seen Oscar a handful of times, even though he had lived on the unit for about a year by then. Sometimes I would see him by the front desk, where his food and water bowls were, or curled up asleep underneath the remains of a tattered old blanket. Oscar did not have a reputation as a sociable cat.

"He's probably just warming up to us a little," I said. "Though I don't profess to be an expert in cats, my experience says they do whatever it is they want to do. He's probably sitting here because he found someone who won't bother him."

"I know this is weird, David, but the thing is, Oscar never really spends any time with the patients. He usually just goes off and hides, mostly in my office. Lately, though, a couple of us here have noticed that he's spending more time with certain residents."

I shrugged. "And why is that weird?" Looking at Oscar curled up beside Mrs. Davis, I was reminded of the cats they buried with the ancient Egyptians. This scene was certainly peaceful enough.

"The thing is," Mary said slowly, "Oscar only spends time with patients who are about to die."

Now I'd heard everything.

"So you're telling me Mrs. Davis is going to die today?" I looked over at her and immediately regretted what I had said.

Her breathing was clearly labored and I felt guilty for my breach in decorum. I realized that Mrs. Davis indeed might die today—a fact that had more to do with her dementia and rapidly progressing cancer than the presence of a cat on her bed.

Mary smiled but I could sense her embarrassment. I felt bad for scoffing at her.

"I suppose it's possible that a cat might know when someone's going to die. Remember that article recently about the cancer-sniffing dogs? And there are those Japanese fish that sense earthquakes before they happen. And what about Lassie? He always knew when Timmy fell down the well."

Mary was not amused. "You know, Oscar wandered into another patient's room right before she died yesterday."

The look on my face must have said it all because Mary stopped trying to convince me. For a moment we both looked in silence at the scene in front of us. The cat, curled up next to Mrs. Davis's leg, was quietly purring.

"Don't get me wrong, Mary," I said, breaking the spell. "I love the concept of an animal sitting with me as I die. It's really quite sweet. I had a dog growing up and he was always by my side."

I walked over by the bed and reached down to pet Oscar. With lightning reflexes he slapped my hand with his front paw. I pulled back, searching for evidence of blood.

"I told you he's not that friendly," Mary said with a smile.

"Friendly! He damn near tried to maul me!" I replied with an air of unnecessary drama.

"Oh, he's okay. Oscar really is affectionate when he wants to be. He just tries to protect his patients."

"Mary, he's a cat—cats don't do anything unless there's something in it for them. He's probably just looking for some empty real estate and a warm blanket to sit on."

I studied my hand some more, looking for the nonexistent scratch.

"God, you're a baby. He barely even touched you."

"The truth is, Mary, I really don't like cats. And from the evidence I can honestly say that I don't think he much likes me either."

Mary laughed. "Cats don't hate you, they just know if you're afraid or not. If you are, they respond accordingly."

"Don't laugh," I said, "but I had a bad experience with a cat while I was a kid and it left me a little traumatized."

For a moment I contemplated telling her the story of my grandmother's cat, but the look of mock sympathy on Mary's face convinced me that it would be better to keep the past in the past.

"Some cats are just ornery," she said breaking the silence. "Some people too, I suppose. But you can't forsake every cat because of one bad experience. Besides, you know we wouldn't have a cat here if there was even the slightest chance it would hurt anybody. Even a doctor!"

"Very funny." I looked back at Oscar and Mrs. Davis. "You know, maybe he likes patients who are dying because they don't give him any trouble."

"I don't know, David. I really think there's something more to it."

"So does that mean that Mrs. Davis is going to die today?"

"I guess we'll see."

• • •

I LEFT THE HOSPITAL and drove across town to my outpatient clinic. Unconsciously I found myself thinking of the cat at my grandmother's cottage. His name was Puma, and appropriately so. In my mind, he was a thirty-pound behemoth of a cat—as any fisherman will tell you, size tends to get larger over time—and for years he terrorized me every time I entered "his house." As I thought of his eyes burning with hatred toward me, I told myself that my fear of cats was not irrational.

Mid-reverie my cell phone rang. It was Mary.

"Mrs. Davis died a few minutes after you left."

It had been less than an hour since I was standing in her room watching her breathe. Even after years of seeing it happen, I still feel a sense of humility at being so close to a death.

"Look, Mary. Don't make too much of that cat business. She was going to die soon anyway. She had two horrible diagnoses."

"Yeah, she did, but I'm telling you that this is happening with some regularity up here. In fact it's pretty much happening every time someone dies. Even some of the residents' families are beginning to talk about it."

She was quiet for moment.

"David," she said, "I really think the cat knows."

CHAPTER TWO

"A man who carries a cat by the tail learns something he can learn in no other way."

MARK TWAIN

HAVE YOU EVER HAD A REALLY BAD DAY, THE KIND THAT makes you question everything you've done and causes you to worry about all that the future holds?

I was having just such a day about six months after my initial encounter with Oscar. I was sitting in my office, staring out of the window. On a clear day my window offers a spectacular view, especially in the summertime when the blue water of Narragansett Bay shimmers beneath a bright sky and marshmallow clouds. In January, though, the view is more likely to be cold and bleak, the water an uninviting slab of asphalt. That's how it looked on that day, and it was a perfect reflection of my state of mind.

My eyes were fixed on a tanker unloading cargo, but I wasn't paying attention. Instead, my mind had been going over the events of the last few days, playing over one scene in particular, like a damaged DVD. Three weeks before, I had learned I was a finalist for a major research award from a prestigious New York foundation. Such grants are more than gravy for me; my research in the field of geriatrics and nursing home medicine is what keeps me going, and receiving an award like this wasn't merely a matter of recognition. I saw it as a validation of everything I did.

Two days earlier I had boarded a train bound for New York. The meeting had gone well, or so I had thought. I left the interview brimming with confidence, and maybe a little pride. This award was mine; I could feel it. I had worked tirelessly on the application, putting in hours late at night after the daily grind of work and family responsibilities. All that midnight oil was going to pay off. The board would see the importance of my work and fund my research, and why shouldn't they? It was crucial and unique and the board must have understood that. On the train back to Providence I had begun plotting how I would use the award as leverage to get my boss to give me the raise I deserved. If I'd had a cigar I would have fired it up (or would have if I smoked and they still let you do that on trains).

But one call had changed all that. The moment the phone had rung that morning I felt a cold stab of dread. There was something about the ring. Perhaps it had come too early. Maybe it was just a premonition. Breathlessly, I had picked up the phone and said hello. The woman on the other end was immediately grim; listening to her, I understood how my patients' families must feel when I call them with bad news.

"We want to thank you for coming to New York to meet with the board. They were very impressed with your work."

The pause that followed was endless.

"But . . . we are sorry to tell you that you were not selected for the funding."

The woman had continued for several moments chirping on about the many "talented candidates" they had interviewed, but I had already stopped listening.

All I could think about was the failure.

No promotion. No raise.

Another career setback.

I felt like the numbers had all been reset and I was back at zero.

Hours after the phone call, I still couldn't get it out of my head. You know the expression "What part of 'no' don't you understand?" I couldn't understand *any* part of it. How could *they* not understand how important this work was? So few people were interested in the nursing home environment and the proposal was good, perhaps the best I'd ever submitted. What could the other candidates possibly be doing that was more important?

Was it my notes?

The way I talked?

My suit?

I tore myself away from the window and forced myself to sit at my desk. I looked at the blinking prompt on my computer. I had been in my office for over an hour and hadn't even logged on. I watched it blink like a failing heart monitor.

Maybe it was my tie?

I picked up the phone to dial the foundation, determined to find out what the problem was. I dialed the number hell-bent on finding someone, anyone, who would listen to my plea for reconsideration.

Suddenly my pager went off. For a moment the world seemed to stop spinning, giving me pause to reconsider my actions. I looked at the numbers on the display.

It was Steere House.

I ignored the page and retreated back to my internal dialogue. Was I really going to learn anything by calling? What part of no did I not understand? Maybe they just weren't interested.

The pager went off again.

Same number.

Don't they know this isn't a good time for me?

Frustrated, I picked up the phone and dialed.

"Hello, Dr. Dosa, how are you?"

"Fine, Mary, what do you need?" There was a distinct edge to my voice.

"Well, someone got up on the wrong side of the bed today. Is something wrong?"

"It's just been a bad day, Mary. What's going on there?"

"Do you want to tell me about it?" she asked sincerely.

I was in no mood to explain myself, let alone apologize. "Not today. But thank you for asking."

"Well, anyway, I wanted to let you know that Ellen Sanders has passed away."

"At least someone is having a worse day than me."

There was a long silence as Mary probably wondered how, or whether, to respond.

I put my hand on my forehead. "I'm really sorry, Mary. That was uncalled for. Pay no attention to me."

"Okay, David." I couldn't tell if Mary was holding her tongue or had just cut me some slack. I knew that she'd had worse days than I could imagine. She tactfully switched gears.

"By the way, I wanted to let you know that Oscar was there."

"Where?"

"At the bedside. Oscar was there when Ellen passed . . . just like all the others lately."

"Come again?"

"You know, our cat friend. Oscar's still making his visits. He's made about five or six since Mrs. Davis died."

On any other day I probably would have just laughed, as I had six months earlier. But there's something about particularly bad days that makes you reconsider your preconceived notions of life. And this was definitely one of those days.

As Mary rattled off some instructions to me about filling out the necessary paperwork, I pictured Oscar sitting next to Ellen and her daughter Kathy.

"Where is he now?" I asked.

"Who? Oscar? Oh, he's still hanging out in Ellen's room. The funeral director hasn't been by yet. In fact, the hospice minister just got here, but Oscar's just sitting on her bed. You know, you should probably give your condolences to Kathy. She really likes you. Why don't you come over and say hello?"

Then she laughed.

"On second thought, given your mood, maybe you should just stay where you are."

I laughed myself. Nothing like the loss of someone else's loved one to put your own problems in perspective. I didn't need to tell Mary this: Her husband took his own life shortly after the birth of their second child, leaving her a single mother who now made the adult children of Steere House her life. My parents were alive and well, my wife and children were healthy—even if my own health was sort of day-to-day. *Carpe diem*, or as the song goes: Get it while you can.

We talked for a few moments about Mrs. Sanders and her family before I rang off. For the first time that morning I thought of someone other than myself.

While Ellen Sanders's death was not surprising, the timing of it was rather unexpected. She had given no indication that she was terminally ill. There were no nasty infections or any of a number of other disease processes that shorten life. Other than her dementia, she was a poster child for good health.

But while none of the medical staff, myself included, thought she was even sick, let alone close to death, that cat sensed something else. While my faith in science and my own intellectual vanity made it easier for me to reject the notion that some errant feline could know more than we as medical staff did, I felt strangely elated by the notion that I could be completely wrong.

Was it a coincidence that Oscar had been there for each patient's death? I thought of that Einstein quote: "Coincidence is God's way of remaining anonymous." Suddenly, I felt the lure of a good mystery. I grabbed my coat and walked over to Steere House, determined to find out more about our mystery cat's behavior.

CHAPTER THREE

"What greater gift than the love of a cat?"

CHARLES DICKENS

WATCHING A LOVED ONE'S HEALTH FAIL IS HARD. MOST families eventually find a way to accept it and move on. Some can even do it with grace and dignity. Mary always spoke of one son who was ceaselessly cheerful in the face of his mother's dementia.

"How do you do it?" she asked him one day.

"Oh, I said good-bye to my mother a long time ago," he told her. "Now I've just fallen in love with this little lady!"

This was an advanced, black belt–level reaction. Maybe it's the guilt, or the fear of death, or simply the heartbreak of seeing the slow decline the disease brings, but many people seem to disappear as their parents or spouses fail, as if they themselves were being diminished.

Not Kathy. Her spirit always seemed indomitable in the face of her mother's condition and she took each slide backward with a glass-half-full optimism that was an inspiration to the staff. She took comfort in the small triumphs, or "little victories," as she called them.

I remembered running into Kathy and her mother seated on a bench in the nursing home's rose garden one afternoon. It was a particularly windy October day and I wondered what on earth they were doing outdoors, huddled in their jackets beside their empty lunch trays.

"Aren't you cold?" I had asked Kathy.

"I prefer to think of it as brisk," she had joked. "You know, for the next three to four months, my mother is going to be cooped up inside. What's a little cold? And look how lovely the leaves are at this time of year."

Kathy had glanced over at her mother and placed an arm around her shoulder.

"Aren't they beautiful, Mom?" she had asked, pointing to the last of the red and gold leaves on a nearby tree. Her mother said nothing, but there was a hint of a smile on her face.

"Little victories, Dr. Dosa," Kathy reminded me as I walked quickly out of the cold that day.

Her last statement echoed through my head as I passed the spot where she and her mother had sat. That October day may very well have been Mrs. Sanders's last time outside.

A sharp winter wind drove me swiftly through the frozen garden and into the nursing home's first-floor dining area. It was almost lunchtime and an aide was busy setting the table. She moved carefully, polishing the silverware as if she were setting up at one of the finest restaurants in town. This attention to detail is part of what makes Steere House unique, I think. Respect for the residents informs nearly every decision here and can be seen in even the simplest of gestures.

In the corner of the dining room, Ida Poirier was sitting patiently in her wheelchair, waiting for lunch to begin. She quietly studied the aide as she polished and placed each piece of silverware. As I entered the dining room, Ida looked up and smiled.

Ida has been a resident of Steere House for many years now, confined to the nursing home because of her rheumatoid arthritis. After years of inflammation, her legs and hands have become a tangled mess, but her mental faculties are as sharp as they've ever been. Despite her predicament, Ida maintained a wry sense of humor that comes from a lifetime of struggling with chronic illness. For the chronically ill the choice seems to be to learn to live with your affliction, and occasionally laugh, or succumb to suffering.

I reached down and gave her a hug.

"What's for lunch today, Ida?"

"Usual crap, Dr. Dosa. I don't know, what is today—Monday, Tuesday?"

"It's Thursday, Ida."

"I think its potpie day, then. Not that it matters; it all tastes the same."

I smiled.

"They try their best, Ida. Unfortunately, they're not working with a budget that allows for filet mignon."

"Maybe not, Dr. Dosa, but could we at least have lobster once in a while? We *are* in Rhode Island, after all."

"I'll talk with the chef."

"Yeah, right!" She shook her head in mock disgust and then tried to gauge my expression. It was nice to have Ida to banter with.

"Dr. Dosa, are you going up to see that patient who died?"

"Why do you ask, Ida?"

"I heard the cat was in there with her when she passed."

I paused before answering. "How did you hear about that?"

"Some of the nurses down here have been talking about Oscar and what he does. Personally, I love cats. I think I've had a cat my whole life. Even now, either Billy or Munchie is always in here keeping me company," she said, referring to the two cats who live on the first floor, "but I don't know about that cat upstairs."

"Do you believe the cat knows?" I asked.

"Oh, I believe it. When my husband died years ago, I bought myself a cat to keep me company. I called him Patches because he had little patches of white on his black fur." She smiled briefly at the memory. "Anyway, Patches always knew whenever I was sick or my arthritis was acting up. He would jump on my bed and just sit with me. Otherwise, I could never seem to find him. He was always hiding somewhere in my apartment—under a bed, in my closet, always somewhere."

"What happened to the cat?"

Ida's expression changed and I regretted asking her.

"He died of some kind of cat cancer. I had to put him down."

"I'm sorry, Ida."

"No, Dr. Dosa, don't feel bad about mentioning it. I had to do it. Sometimes I think we're kinder to animals than we are to people . . ." She looked out the window in silence. It was more than a little awkward, but I let it play out.

"You know," she said, eventually breaking the spell, "every day, I sit here and wait. I wait for someone to help me get dressed. I wait for breakfast, then for lunch. After that, it's back to my room for a nap or to watch some stupid soap or talk show on TV. Then I wait for dinner. When I was young, I never had time. I was always on the go, didn't have a minute for myself. Now, all I have is time."

She looked off in the distance again, lost in her thoughts. When she turned back to me I sensed her mood had changed again.

"Dr. Dosa, I almost envy that patient upstairs. At least she is free of all of this."

For emphasis, she held up her hands as if presenting evidence. Her fingers, bent inward at impossible angles, rendered her hands useless.

"I used to love to knit. I'd sit for hours in my sunroom and knit scarves or blankets. It didn't matter who I was knitting for. Sometimes I'd knit blankets for one of my cats. Other times, I'd take them to the Women's Hospital across the street for the newborns. I can't even do that anymore."

Frustrated, she dropped her hands into her lap. I looked at her and racked my brain for something to say that might lessen her sorrow. I had nothing to offer.

"I really miss him," Ida said abruptly. "The cat, I mean," she added. "I miss Patches."

I put my hand on her shoulder and we sat together in companionable silence. She acknowledged my touch with a smile, but I couldn't help thinking that she probably wished I were a cat.

"Dr. Dosa, animals have this sixth sense and they can communicate with us if we understand their language. I'm telling you that Patches wouldn't leave my side if I was sick."

"You mentioned your other cats. What about them? Were they like Patches?"

Ida smiled again. "No, Ginger was friendly as can be. She was always at my feet or on my lap, but she really didn't have that sense of when I needed her. Now Grover, he was—"

"You named your cat Grover?"

"I let my niece name him. I probably should have called him Oscar the Grouch, though, because he could be meaner than a rattlesnake."

"So you believe all of this about the cat upstairs?"

Ida looked up at me with a knowing smile.

"You're not much of a cat person, are you?"

"I can't say that I am, but I'm trying to be."

Then Ida openly laughed.

"I knew it! I could tell you were more of a dog person. You're too damn nice."

Her humor was contagious and I found myself laughing from deep within. I needed that. "Thank you, Ida. I'm not sure you meant it as a compliment but I'll take it today."

"You're welcome."

She studied my expression again.

"Something's wrong," she said finally. "There's something you're not telling me."

"It's just been a bad day, Ida."

She smiled. "You'll have a lot more of those in your life. Forget about it. Most of the time it's not as bad as you think it is. Just go home, kiss your wife and kids, drink a beer, go to bed early, and you'll feel better in the morning!"

"Doctor's orders?" I asked her.

"Doctor's orders!"

RIDING THE ELEVATOR to the third floor, I thought of Ida's sharp mind and damaged hands and I felt troubled. If I was being truthful—and this did seem to be a day of truths, welcome or not—what bothered me about Ida was a connection we shared. Looking at her sometimes I felt that I was staring at my own future. I glanced down at my own hands and studied my enlarged left thumb. It was ten years since I myself was diagnosed with an inflammatory arthritis very similar to Ida's. I looked at my swollen right wrist and thought of the swelling in my left knee and ankle. The joints were not as painful as they once were, thanks to my complicated medical regimen of pills and injections. Yet the telltale signs of inflammation were there and I knew that, like Ida, my joints would fail me, my own legs would not carry me into my proverbial golden years, and my own arms might not be able to hold my grandchildren.

I felt a shiver as I thought about Ida and the curse of not being able to do the things you once liked to do. I allowed the feeling to wash over me, felt the self-pity rise and fall like a fever, and then shrugged it off. Instead, I thought of Kathy and what she had said about the importance of little daily victories in combating chronic illness. I've had over a decade to think about chronic illness in my own life and know that she is right. There are more important things in life than careers and grants. There are the day-to-day victories, the gifts of the here and now. Instead of worrying about my old age and my grandchildren, couldn't I just rejoice in being able to carry my newborn daughter up the stairs and play soccer with my son? I was still able to bend over and tie my own shoes. Tomorrow's problems would have to wait.

I exited the elevator onto the third floor, stepping directly into a meeting between several aides and a hospice nurse at the front desk. They were in the midst of an intense conversation, one that I quickly realized revolved around Oscar.

"So he did it again," I interjected.

"Yes, he did," Lisa, the hospice nurse, replied. "He's developing quite a unique talent."

We were joined at the front desk by Sally, one of the hospice ministers. She had just returned from Mrs. Sanders's room.

"How is Kathy doing?" I asked her.

"She's upset, but I think she'll do fine eventually. She's had a long time to come to grips with today."

I left them and walked down the hall to Mrs. Sanders's room. Kathy was holding her mother's hand, crying quietly, while Oscar sprawled out on the bed, his front and hind legs extended, his spine resting gently against Mrs. Sanders's leg. Kathy turned to greet me. Beneath her swollen eyes she managed a slight smile and rose to give me a hug.

"I'm sorry," I said.

She began to cry again and I felt her warm tears through my shirt. We held the embrace until it became uncomfortable. Kathy's eyes were bloodshot and she looked like she hadn't slept in days. Her blouse was wet from her tears and wrinkled from the vigil she passed in the chair beside her mother's bed. I tried to think of something to say that might make her loss easier but came up blank again. Thankfully, Kathy broke the silence.

"Dr. Dosa, I want to thank you for everything you have done for my mother."

She wiped her eyes with her sleeves and turned to sit back down in her seat by the bed. She picked up her mother's hand again and cradled it in her own. The movement stirred Oscar, who looked rather tired himself. He blinked and looked at Kathy.

"Can you believe this cat?" Kathy said.

"I heard that he was here when your mother died," I replied. Through her tears she smiled slightly.

"Yeah, he and I are buddies now," she said and reached over to pet Oscar on the head. Oscar accepted the attention and nuzzled Kathy's hand.

"The hospice nurse and the minister told me he's done this before," she said.

"For the last year or so, from what I'm told," I replied.

"Well, he's a really special cat."

"I suppose . . . ," I said, and realized that a small part of me was starting to believe it.

I put my hand on Mrs. Sanders's hand and said a private good-bye to my patient. Neither Kathy nor I spoke. On the bed next to us, Oscar sat quietly purring. Finally, after several minutes, I asked the question I'd been contemplating since my conversation with Mary.

"Kathy, were you okay with Oscar being here at the end?"

She looked at me for a moment and then said, "Dr. Dosa, I think of Oscar as my angel. He was here for my mother, and here for me, too. With Oscar at my side . . . well, I felt a little less alone. It's hard to explain, but some animals, well, the sense they give you is that they understand what's going on. More than that, they just accept. I don't know, but Oscar gave me a feeling that this is all natural. And it is, isn't it? If birth is a miracle, isn't death a miracle too? My mother . . . well, her struggle is finally over. She's finally free."

Kathy stared at me, waiting for a response, but I gave her no indication of what I was thinking. I guess I really didn't know.

"My mother never wanted to live the way she did in the end," she added. "She was a proud woman. You didn't know her before, but she had a tremendous sense of pride. She always dressed fashionably and she was quick with a joke."

She smiled, perhaps remembering one of her mother's jokes, one that she did not share with me.

Looking at Kathy, I realized that she would be fine. The coming days would be hard on her, but she would move on to the next chapter in her life—one that wouldn't involve daily trips to Steere House.

I said one last good-bye to Kathy and realized that our association had come to an end.

"Take care of yourself," I said.

Kathy nodded as I left and returned to her thoughts, and to Oscar.

CHAPTER FOUR

"Cats are connoisseurs of comfort."

JAMES HERRIOT

WHEN I RETURNED TO STEERE HOUSE A FEW DAYS LATER I found Mary seated at the nurse's desk brushing Oscar. Sprawled out in full glory, he looked like a boxer after a major bout—or, given his mane, one of those big-time wrestlers.

"The last couple of days Oscar's seemed pretty beat from his vigil," Mary said.

"Sure . . . sitting on a bed sleeping is really hard work."

"You laugh, David, but Oscar's always tired after the fact. It's like he's on the clock when someone is dying and then afterward he's spent."

I rolled my eyes, something that annoys Mary as much as it does my wife.

"Domesticated cats were like dogs, you know," she said, as she continued her ministrations. "They had to earn their keep on the farm. Maybe this is like Oscar's job."

"Well, I need to start doing my job," I said, opening a chart that I had spent the better part of ten minutes looking for. As any nurse or doctor can tell you, the chart you need is invariably the one that is missing. Anyway, I must have made it look awfully inviting because suddenly Oscar left Mary's side and jumped up onto the counter next to me. Then he twirled around twice before sitting down in a clump of fur on my paperwork.

"Will you look at that," I said in anguish.

"It's a cat's world," said Mary. "We just work in it."

I grabbed the chart out from under Oscar, who glared at me.

"You're gonna make me sit somewhere else, aren't you?"

Mary laughed.

"David, you never win an argument with a cat. Don't you know that by now?"

She got up from her seat and motioned for me to sit down. "Here. I've gotta go down and see Ruth Rubenstein anyway."

"Anything going on with her that I need to know about?"

"I don't know yet, but Mr. Rubenstein wants to see me."

"Do you need reinforcements?" I inquired, drawing a smile.

"No, I think I'll be all right . . . but you might want to keep your pager handy in case I need you later."

As Mary disappeared down the hall, I thought back to the first time I had met the Rubensteins.

I LOVE MY JOB, even though it's sometimes less than satisfying. Often I'm the bearer of bad news, the detective with the inconvenient truth. Too often the suspects work in pairs, covering for each other: mother and daughter a lot of the time, or, in the case of the Rubensteins, husband and wife. If they work together to keep me out of their lives—even when they come to me looking for help—it's because I'm the messenger, the one with the bad news. I'm the one who confirms what they often already know deep inside. There's simply no easy way to tell someone they have cancer, heart disease, emphysema, or any other horrible disease that takes so much before it results in death. But it's particularly hard to tell someone they have dementia, even when the person intuitively knows it already.

That's what I had to do with the Rubensteins some three years before. I had to look into the eyes of the eighty-year-old woman I had just examined and ruin her life. I knew from experience that her husband would be sitting with her, a deer-in-the-headlights look on his face. I knew this look and it said that I am their judge, jury, and executioner. To a certain extent, he would be right. I thought of the end of the mouse's tale in *Alice in Wonderland*: "'I'll be judge, I'll be jury,' said cunning old Fury: 'I'll try the whole cause and condemn you to death.'"

Earlier on the day that I first met the Rubensteins I'd been with Mr. Earl, a delightful eighty-five-year-old with few medical problems and a mind that ran at full throttle. During his physical exam he told me in great detail about the book he was reading. Then he regaled me with stories of his recent volunteer work with a local nonprofit and his plans to travel to Florida for the winter. When my exam was finished I sat down with him. Even though I was running a little behind, I wanted to let him go on for a few more minutes before I moved toward the door, the indication that our time was over. He took my gesture with good grace and apologized for taking up more of my time than he intended to.

"Mr. Earl," I said, waving off his apology, "I hope I am as healthy as you are when I get to be your age." I knew I wouldn't be—I already had more health problems in my thirties than he had—but I said it anyway.

He smiled. "I'm a lucky man, Dr. Dosa. The trick is eight hours of sleep, a healthy diet, and lots of lovin'!"

Who can argue with that?

Donna Richards, my office manager, confronted me as soon as I stepped into the hallway. She was looking at her watch and seemed a little frazzled.

"Are you done yet?" she asked.

I nodded.

"You have a new patient in room 3 who is getting restless. Her husband has already been out to ask where the doctor is. I've played interference, but you've got to speed it up."

I told her I was doing the best I could. Of all people, Donna should know how hard it is to appropriately care for older patients and give them the time they deserve. Her own mother was a patient in our clinic.

I grabbed the next chart and took a moment to look over some paperwork from another local doctor before I knocked on the door. The well-dressed couple I found did not look pleased. The man held up his watch and tapped it several times with his finger.

"You know, Dr. Dosa, our appointment was for 2:15 PM. You are twenty minutes late."

"Mr. and Mrs. Rubenstein, I'm so sorry to keep you. Please accept my apology."

Going to the doctor is not like getting your shoes shined and, unfortunately, there are times when other patients need my attention for longer than I anticipated. But I've learned over the years that explanations only make things worse. Simple apologies work better. Not in this case, though.

Frank Rubenstein was insulted, not on his behalf, I soon realized, but on his wife's. He was a gentleman of the old school, and rather old world, at that. I recognized his Eastern European accent as being not so distant from that of my own parents, and I thought I recognized the attitude too.

Concern takes many forms, I've come to learn as a doctor, and it's easier to recognize when it comes as a purr than a growl. Frank was like a papa lion protecting his lioness from predators, real or imagined. I posed no threat to his wife—I was simply there in front of them at the wrong time. What was really stalking her came from within.

Ruth Rubenstein, who was sitting across from him, seemed mildly embarrassed.

"Oh, Doctor, I'm so sorry for my husband's brutish behavior. I'm sure you have lots of other patients to attend to. Frank just doesn't like coming to the doctor's office."

She flashed me a disarming smile and then turned quickly to glare at her husband. He got the message; they'd been together long enough. As Ruth stared down her husband, I took a moment to look her over. She was neatly dressed in a long skirt and white blouse. She was strikingly attractive with blue-green eyes that radiated warmth. Her long silver hair was arresting, pulled back behind her ears with what looked to be an expensive pearl hairpin. Her skin still had a youthful vigor, and my first thought was that this woman still had it together.

I offered her my hand. She grasped it firmly and I was overpowered by her perfume.

My heart sank.

I moved in closer and confirmed my initial suspicion. Beneath the scent of her cologne I recognized the unmistakable musty odor of urine, a sign of incontinence.

I introduced myself again and asked how I could help them. Mr. Rubenstein launched into an explanation.

"Doctor, as you've probably figured, neither of us particularly want to be here, but I'm concerned about my wife's health."

He looked down at the floor, collecting his thoughts.

"I'm concerned . . ." His voice trailed off as if he was searching for a delicate way of telling me about his wife's problem.

"Go on," I said, nodding. He looked back at me, having found his voice.

"My wife has started to do some strange things. She loses things. The other day, she couldn't find her keys. She blamed me. Eventually I found them in the refrigerator with the groceries she had just brought home. She's also gotten lost a couple of times coming back from the grocery store. One time she called me and she was halfway across town."

He looked over at Mrs. Rubenstein, who acted as if we were talking about someone else. She just stared at the cover of the magazine in her lap.

Frank continued. He was likely the same age as his wife, although he appeared significantly older. He was dressed in a vintage suit, circa 1970. No doubt he was the original owner. His hairline had receded and whatever hair remained was uncombed. As he told me more stories about Ruth's memory lapses—the day she forgot to meet him for coffee or the morning she put the milk in the cupboard—I looked back over at

Ruth. Now she was attending to his words, and if looks could kill, he was the one who would have needed medical attention.

When Frank finished speaking, I asked Ruth conversational questions geared at assessing her memory. She skillfully deflected many of them, often deferring to her husband. There's an almost symbiotic relationship between couples that have been married a long time; the Rubensteins were no different. When I asked Ruth to tell me about her favorite restaurant she responded by playfully asking her husband to answer the question.

"Darling, what was the name of that restaurant we ate at the other night?"

"The Golden Palace, Ruth."

"Yes, Doctor, have you eaten there?" she asked.

I shook my head no.

"You really must try it. We really love that restaurant. They have the best meals."

"What do you like to eat there?" I asked her, doing my Columbo routine.

"Oh, I like everything."

"What did you eat last time you were there?"

Ruth stared at me blankly. I imagined her flipping through her mental calendar and finding every page blank. Eventually she looked to her husband for assistance.

"We had the Peking duck, Doctor."

"That's right, the Peking duck." Ruth seemed pleased with herself, as if she was the one who had recovered the memory. "It was so good. You really have to try it."

I smiled and said I would. The conversation, however, was troubling. Despite her preserved social graces, it was becoming increasingly apparent that Ruth had some issues with her short-term memory at the very least. Though she skillfully hid it by deferring to her husband, the more I continued to isolate her from his coaching, the more apparent it became. The simple memory tests I gave her next only confirmed my suspicions.

I gave Ruth a piece of paper and a pen.

"I'm going to ask you to draw me a large circle and pretend it is a clock. Please put the numbers on the clock."

It's a simple task that any grade school student should be able to perform, but Ruth struggled with it. Robbed of her husband's assistance, she painstakingly placed the numbers on the clock, pausing to consider the position of each one as if her very life depended on it. Perhaps, in a way, it did. After a minute, she looked up at me with a sense of accomplishment. Like a student proudly giving an aced test to a parent, she handed me the piece of paper. I looked down at her work and noted that the numbers one through twelve had been placed correctly on the clock. Then I handed the paper back to her.

"Now I want you to draw the hands on there at 2:45."

My request was met with a concerned smile. Ruth's eyes drifted up toward the clock above the doorway. She studied it momentarily before speaking.

"Doctor, I don't know how any of this has anything to do with me. I'm fine, really. I don't know what my husband is going on about."

"Mrs. Rubenstein, I know it seems silly, but the test can really be helpful to me in figuring out what is going on. Could you just place the hands of the clock at 2:45, please?"

Ruth sized me up.

I refused to back down.

She looked back at her drawing and shook her head, as if frustrated by the inconsequential nature of my request. She considered the numbers on the page.

"What time do you want?"

"2:45."

Over the next minute, the mental strain of the activity became more obvious. She tapped her pen on the paper. Intermittently she broke the silence with nervous laughter.

"I was never really good at math," she announced. I didn't have the heart to tell her that the task had more to do with visual-spatial skills and executive function than math. The clock test is standard for just that reason: If you can do it, the chances are excellent you don't have Alzheimer's. It's also a highly significant indicator of how you will do on the road. I wish the DMV would give this test along with the eye exam.

I waited patiently for Ruth to finish. Finally, after several minutes, she drew the little hand pointing to the 2. Then, like thousands of other patients with memory impairment, Ruth placed the minute hand of the clock between the 4 and 5, rather than at the 9.

Convinced that she had once again aced her exam, Ruth looked up at me with a sense of extreme satisfaction. As I looked over at her husband, it was apparent that he didn't share her enthusiasm. A tear had come to his eyes, which he quickly wiped away before it could find its way down his check.

I then launched immediately into another battery of memory tests without saying a word about her performance. She seemed momentarily disappointed by the lack of feedback, but there is nothing much that I can say in that situation—nothing that the patient wants to hear, anyway.

"All right, Mrs. Rubenstein, I'm going to say three words and ask you to commit them to memory."

I recited three words—*apple*, *book*, and *coat*—and asked her to repeat them back to me. She remembered two out of three. Five minutes later, she would almost certainly remember none.

I asked her to spell a five-letter word, *world,* forward. She did so, quickly and precisely. A smile that said "I told you there is nothing wrong with me" appeared on her face.

"Now can you spell it backward?" I asked.

She looked at me with the sort of lethal stare she gave her husband earlier.

"Doctor, I don't understand why any of this is necessary. I'm totally fine."

I repeated my request and she continued to struggle; she was finally able to get only two of the five letters in place.

Switching gears to another memory test, I asked her to write down the names of as many four-legged animals as she could in a minute. Normally, patients can name over ten in this test of executive function. Today, my five-year-old son could probably name twice that, but Ruth named only six that day and wrote *cat* down twice.

We finished a few additional tests and I asked Frank to escort me to the waiting area so I could conduct a more thorough physical examination. He seemed reluctant to leave, but did so grudgingly after his wife gave him a reassuring smile.

"It's okay, dear. It's just part of the exam," she said.

In the hallway, I used the opportunity to openly ask Frank some harder questions about his wife. I have learned over the years that there are many things family members do not want to disclose in front of the person suspected of having dementia.

"Has she done anything dangerous?" I asked.

"What do you mean, Doctor?"

"Has she left the bathtub running or has she left the stove on?"

"I suppose she's burned the meatloaf a couple of times but she was never much of a cook."

He attempted a meek smile.

"Has she crashed the car or been in any fender benders?"

Patients with dementia have an extremely high rate of car accidents although few are ever reported. Frank shook his head.

"Has she acted strangely or have you noticed her behavior changing?"

"She's a little more suspicious than she used to be. The other day, I went out to a restaurant with a few friends. When I got home, I caught her going through my wallet. When I asked her what she was doing, she accused me of being with another woman. Doctor, you have to understand that I would never *ever* do something like that!"

I nodded again and told Frank to sit in the waiting room. I returned to the examination room to complete Mrs. Rubenstein's physical. She had changed into the paper gown and was sitting on the examination table waiting for me.

"Doctor, I really think I am okay."

She looked at me for any evidence of an opinion to the contrary. I have learned not to give anything away: if I played poker I could probably make a killing.

"What did my husband say to you out there?" she asked me. "I don't know why he's so concerned about me."

I smiled.

"He loves you, Mrs. Rubenstein, and he is concerned about your health. By the way, how long have you been married?"

She looked at me and then beamed.

"Too long, Doctor. We met in Europe during the war."

"Oh, yeah? What was that thirty, forty, or fifty years ago?" I was pushing her for an exact number.

She shrugged her shoulders. "Too long, Doctor, too long!"

I smiled at her, wondering to myself if I would ever get to the point where I wouldn't remember how long I'd been married. I know that Ruth's attempt at humor was just a ruse to hide the fact that she really had no idea. She could have been married ten years or a hundred.

"I have to admit, Mrs. Rubenstein, that I share some of your husband's concerns regarding your memory."

She shook her head and reached over to put her hand on mine as a gesture of reassurance.

"Oh, Doctor, I'm just tired. I really have a lot on my mind."

"That might be the case, Ruth, but I am a little worried that there may be more going on. Would you let me order some more tests?"

"But, Doctor, why would you want to order more tests? Tests for what?"

I couldn't keep beating around the bush.

"Ruth, I'd feel better if you'd allow me to order a few more tests."

She shrugged and offered grudging approval. "If you think it's really necessary."

"Ruth, how long has your husband been concerned about your memory?"

She became defensive.

"I don't know, Doctor. He keeps telling me that my memory is not as good as it used to be. Well, of course it's not as good as it used to be." She pointed at herself, smiling. "Look at me: I'm an old lady!"

I laughed at her candor. If nothing else, she still had a sense of humor. But it's a common misconception: Age really has *nothing* to do with memory, and problems with memory are *never* normal aging. People assume the two are related because memory problems become more common as we age. Yet memory impairment is *always* abnormal and should be worked up.

"You're not that old," I said. "You could actually pass for twenty years younger!"

"Well, thank you, Doctor," she said, and I think she actually blushed.

I decided not to make any further comments until I brought Frank back into the room. I finished her physical exam and excused myself to allow her to get dressed.

By the time I returned with her husband, in a matter of mere moments, her mood had changed. I looked directly at Ruth and could see the quiet desperation in her face.

"Doctor, all of these memory tests that you did. They're all silly. I'm okay—right? I just have a lot on my mind these days."

But her eyes said something else. She knew there was a problem. People usually do.

I couldn't meet the gaze and looked instead at the floor between us.

Now they knew.

Sometimes there are tears when I deliver bad news. This time there was only silence. I'd rather have tears. At least you can do something. You can reach over and grab a box of tissues from the counter. You can place a reassuring hand on someone's shoulder.

Silence is the worst.

In medical school, they used to teach you to be detached but empathetic when giving bad news. *Listen and support but don't get involved.*

Easier said than done.

I'm human and I get to know my patients. I meet their families and hear about their children and grandchildren. I get to celebrate their successes and be there for them during the difficult times. It is the part of the job that I find most intoxicating—working to develop a trusting doctor-patient relationship where my patients can feel comfortable sharing everything. A doctor's office should feel like a safe place, an arena in which you can bring out your demons or your angels, your deepest fears and most intimate secrets. In return I have to be honest. That can be the worst part of my job.

"I'm sorry, Mrs. Rubenstein. The memory testing that we did shows there are parts of your memory that are not working as well as they used to. These tests I'd like to run will give us a better sense of what's going on."

The blank expressions on their faces told me they didn't understand.

"Mrs. Rubenstein, I think you have a type of dementia, the medical term we use when you have a problem with memory."

Silence. No tears. I could hear the second hand tick on the clock over the door, the same clock she glanced at when taking her test.

It was Frank who eventually broke the silence. "Is it Alzheimer's, Doctor?" he asked. Suddenly he was the captain of a rudderless ship on an uncharted ocean. He was flying without instruments, driving without a map.

"I'd like to order a few more tests, Mr. Rubenstein, but Alzheimer's is the most common form of dementia and the memory tests I've performed thus far are consistent with that diagnosis."

Frank nodded grimly. Since they had no other questions, I began to tell them about Alzheimer's disease and how it affects brain cells. I told them the disease would ultimately result in further memory loss and perhaps even behavior changes. I tried to console them by saying that there are a few medications that might delay her symptoms and that her deterioration will be gradual at best. I informed them that she should exercise regularly, something that has recently been shown to improve memory. I concluded by telling them that in all likelihood, she might one day die *with* dementia rather than *of* it.

Small consolation to someone who has just been told her life will never be the same. *Their* lives.

The discussion left both husband and wife visibly shaken. A minute passed and I finally broke the spell, asking them if they had any further questions. They shook their heads. I left the room and walked toward my office.

"Doctor!"

Frank had followed me down the hall to ask the one question that everyone wants to know.

"How long does she have?"

"Truthfully, Mr. Rubenstein, I really don't know."

"But Doctor, surely you have some idea of how long she has."

Pressed on the issue, I offered a guess.

"She has relatively early dementia currently but based on where her memory is today, I suspect that she has perhaps three to five years before she loses the ability to care for herself."

My response was met with a look of nonbelief, followed quickly by anger. It was as if I was the one who had brought her the disease rather than the diagnosis.

All he needed was a gun to shoot the messenger.

As I said, sometimes I hate my job.

CHAPTER FIVE

"One cat just leads to another."

ERNEST HEMINGWAY

A LARGE PORTRAIT OF HENRY STEERE HANGS OVER THE piano in the lobby. It's a cozy setting, what with the sunlight streaming through in midafternoon. But that wasn't what I thought the first time I heard the piano playing. When I had wandered into the lobby on my first visit to Steere House, piano music filled the space with a Chopin prelude, but there was no one else in the room. I had looked over expecting to see one of the more able residents or a family member seated before the keys practicing. Instead, there were only Billy and Munchie, the two resident lobby cats, staring back at me from the comfort of an otherwise unoccupied piano bench. The oddness of the scene, two cats seated at a piano bench while music filled the air, was overwhelming—until I realized it was a player piano.

Today I was stealing a few minutes of downtime before rounds. I had settled myself into one of the lobby's comfy chairs and was enjoying the music. I guess I was reflecting, too, on the need to soften the reality of a nursing home—the last home most of our patients will know. At Steere House, perhaps we've achieved the same effect with a family of cats, an atrium of glass, and the sounds of classical music played by the best pianist you never saw.

As if on cue, one of the lobby cats rubbed against my legs. It was Munchie. He's an unusual-looking fellow: grayish-black with spatters of chestnut and brown, like an expressionist painting gone wrong. He meowed loudly, calling out for affection. Cautiously, I reached over and stroked him behind the ears. That flipped the purring switch and he continued to bang against my legs like a bumper car.

"You're not so bad," I said. "At least you don't attack me, like some cats I could mention."

Munchie looked up at me and then curled up over my feet, fully obscuring them from view. As he settled in for a nap, a more ordinary-looking black-and-white cat appeared and jumped into my lap. Billy turned twice before curling up in a ball. Then he looked at me as if to say, "You didn't think you were going to get away without petting me, too, did you?" My pager rang, and I frowned. How do cats always seem to know when you have to be somewhere else?

"Sorry, guys," I said as I stood up. "Mary's paging me and I suspect that I've got to check in on Mrs. Rubenstein upstairs." Munchie scurried away and Billy leaped off my lap and looked at me with that air of disdain only cats can muster. Feeling guilty for having shortchanged him, I leaned over and gave him some gentle petting. But he lost interest after only a few seconds and wandered off to find his friend. Calling a cat fickle is like saying snow's wet.

As I left the lobby I looked back at the cats in the atrium; they were already engaged in chasing each other, like two kids playing tag. My comings and goings were of no concern to them. They were truly in the now. My life is made of pagers, deadlines, appointments, and responsibilities. At that moment the existence of a cat looked pretty good to me.

I got on the elevator and, as if by reflex, found myself looking to the back corner, half expecting to see Steere House's very first cat, Henry, curled up on the floor. It's Henry and his successors that make Steere House so different from other nursing homes; it's a menagerie of cats, rabbits, and birds.

It wasn't always this way, though. Before the 1980s there was no such thing as pet therapy. Animals didn't have a place in health care institutions. Why bring a "dirty animal" into a sterile environment? Then some scientists began to espouse the human-animal bond theory—the belief that animals can have a beneficial effect on human health and psychology. Research increasingly began to back up this belief. Nursing home patients in particular—with or without memory loss—were less depressed and lonely with animal companions. I suppose intuitively this makes sense. Most people love animals. Why wouldn't they want them in their last home?

I'd like to tell you that Steere House's acceptance of animals came about as a result of this research, but truth to tell, I think it was all due to a little guy named Henry. He was literally Steere House's first occupant—and the one the nursing home tried hardest to get rid of.

Since its foundation over a century ago, Steere House has gone through several incarnations, growing to suit the needs of the community. As the current structure was being built, workers noticed that a stray cat had wandered onto the construction site and was living in the unfinished building. The cat was even known to steal from an unattended lunchbox or two. By the time the building was completed, the cat had seemingly moved on and was forgotten. Shortly after the dedication ceremony for the modern Steere House, however, the cat returned to give the building his own inspection. Early one morning he strolled back into the facility, liked what he saw, and sat down in an easy chair. At first the staff tried to shoo the animal away, to no avail. Each day the cat returned, undaunted, through the lobby's sliding glass doors. His attitude was one of entitlement. "I was here first," he seemed to suggest with each wave of his tail.

Like my earlier run-in with Oscar over desk space, the administrator at the time also failed to win his argument with a cat. Eventually the cat's persistence paid off and the staff gave up on chasing him out of the building. A meeting was held and the leadership at Steere House decided to accept their unwanted guest. But he needed a name. It seemed only fitting that he be named after the building's benefactor, Henry Steere, whose likeness looked down upon the very chair that our Henry favored during those early days.

So Henry stayed, and for the next ten years he became a favorite of staff and residents alike. Until his final days he was known to ride the elevators up and down, constantly on the prowl for a cozy place to sprawl in a warm pool of sunshine. But as with all the other residents of Steere House, age eventually caught up with Henry. In his last year of life he began to lose his vision. As a result the poor thing started to walk into walls or closed doors. Over time Henry's behavior also became increasingly erratic. He would wander out of the facility and get lost outdoors. Search parties would be organized and the cat that was once chased away was now ironically returned to the facility. On some days he would simply walk into the elevator, curl up in the corner, and ride between floors all day long, going up and down hundreds of times.

"Do you know there is a cat just sitting in the corner of your elevator?" visitors would ask.

The staff would respond with a smile and gentle reassurance that it was just "Henry being Henry." In truth, many members of the staff had privately started to wonder if Henry had developed dementia like so many of the human residents he lived with. Increasingly, his behavior seemed to confirm this diagnosis.

At the end of his days, Henry had trouble eating, became incontinent, and even started to lose weight. Some in the facility began to question whether he should be euthanized. Several members of the staff lovingly doubled their efforts to care for him in order to stave off a one-way trip to the veterinarian. I suppose it's only fitting that the staff refused to stop caring for their ailing cat. Henry was no different than many of the patients they cared for on a daily basis.

Thankfully, the staff never had to make the difficult decision of putting him down. As if to do them all a favor, Henry went to bed one night and never woke up. A funeral was conducted several days after; almost everyone, staff and residents alike, was there. It was the kind of send-off you would expect for a head of state. Someone gave a eulogy; another member of the staff had even crafted a handmade coffin out of wood.

When the service was over and people were still drying their eyes, Henry was laid to rest on the grounds behind the facility.

Henry changed the culture at Steere House. Thanks to him, the nursing home became increasingly animal-friendly and perhaps more of a home. Sensing the loss of their pet, members of the staff and several more able residents began to vehemently petition the nursing home leadership to replace Henry. Though resistant at first, the chief administrator gave in and staff began to scout out potential replacements. Oscar and Maya were eventually adopted from separate newspaper advertisements and came to reside on the third floor. Billy and Munchie were rescue cats whose owner had died. A hospice nurse brought them into the facility. Finally, Chico and Molly were adopted for the lower-acuity dementia unit on the first floor. All told, six cats were brought in to replace Henry, along with a handful of other animals. They were brought here because of an unwanted cat that didn't want to leave.

Maybe we started adding cats to make this house feel more like a home. But I was starting to think they were the ones teaching us that what makes a home is a family.

CHAPTER SIX

"The real measure of a day's heat is the length of a sleeping cat."

CHARLES J. BRADY

WHEN A PATIENT IS TERMINAL, DOCTORS WILL TALK about limiting care. These conversations go beyond discussions about CPR and whether or not to resuscitate the patient if his heart stops or breathing fails. In most cases, these conversations involve difficult questions about withholding tests and treatments, and whether further medical care should be limited to comfort care.

In cases where the patient has a terminal illness such as cancer, comfort-care discussions are relatively concrete. A patient often has pain or nausea. She may be losing weight rapidly and finds she no longer has an appetite. She may be yellow from jaundice. At times, her organs might even be failing. As difficult as all this is, these signs and symptoms are concrete; it's easy for a physician to talk about them with family members. The idea of treating further pain, even at the expense of length of life, is acceptable to most people. It's what we do when there are no other treatments to offer.

The same cannot be said for dementia.

Although diseases such as Alzheimer's are also considered terminal, they manifest themselves much more slowly. Like erosion that changes the landscape of a beach, the effects of these diseases are measured over months and years rather than days. Because it's usually not pain or discomfort that the patient is suffering, the discussions are more complex and ethically abstract. Care providers and families are forced to grapple with decisions like withholding antibiotics for a potentially curable pneumonia or deciding when it's no longer appropriate to conduct further diagnostic testing for an everyday condition like anemia or weight loss. In turn, doctors must also grapple with the question of whether a diagnostic workup for an everyday problem makes sense. Will I do anything even if the patient has cancer or some other disease? If not, why order the test?

Where Alzheimer's is concerned the roller-coaster ride of acute illnesses followed by partial recoveries can also leave families with a false sense of hope. I've had family members tell me, "If we can just cure the pneumonia, I know Mom will get better." "If we can just get Dad over this hump, I'm sure we'll see some progress." Families become preoccupied with the notion that if the patient is sent to the hospital and cured of his pneumonia (or his staph infection, or his broken hip), he'll eventually be healed. Lost is the fact that the chronic disease progresses steadily despite the recovery from the acute event, leaving the patient considerably weaker and less prepared to deal with the next challenge.

But finding a place to draw the line in patients with dementia can become challenging and fraught with ethical dilemmas for both the next of kin and the health care provider. It was that way with Frank and Ruth Rubenstein.

• • •

"Dr. Dosa, I need you to see my wife right now."

The assertiveness in Frank's voice sent Oscar, resting peacefully on the countertop, scurrying for cover. He found it under the desk between Mary's legs. If I had been quicker, I very well might have joined him.

"What can I help you with, Mr. Rubenstein?"

"It's Ruth. She's more confused today than she was yesterday. And she's not eating. I'm worried about her."

"Let me finish with a few things here at the desk and I'll be down in a minute."

My response was met with a glare and for a moment, I thought he might wait at the desk for me to finish whatever it was I had to do, but he turned away eventually, muttering something under his breath. I had to remind myself that he was concerned about his wife and that his concern was manifesting itself as, well, old-man grumpiness.

"So, do you want to tell me what this is all about?" I asked, turning to Mary as he disappeared.

"Ruth's not doing so well lately, David. She's not eating and she's dropped a few pounds. I suppose he's worried that we're not taking her weight loss seriously enough."

"How much weight are we talking about?"

"About ten pounds."

I frowned. The irony is that so many of my patients could *stand* to lose ten pounds to help with their diabetes, hypertension, or cholesterol but not Mrs. Rubenstein. The 5'2" lady was probably 110 pounds sopping wet the day she entered the nursing home. Ten pounds was a big deal.

"Do you think anything else is going on?"

Mary shrugged. "I suppose anything is possible, but I honestly think her dementia is just getting worse. By the way, he's asked for a referral to a gastroenterologist. He's worried she has colon cancer."

In a healthy patient, the idea of seeing a gastroenterologist for a colonoscopy to evaluate weight loss would certainly be indicated, but with Ruth's rapid mental decline, the prospect of subjecting her to multiple tests and procedures was probably not in her best interests.

"Have we started any discussions with Frank about limiting his wife's care?"

"David, I don't get hazard pay here."

I sighed as I looked at Oscar curled up in a ball in a nook under the desk.

"You got any space down there for me?"

"Nice try, David. I talked to him last time. It's your turn to go talk to the man."

MY FIRST MEETING with the Rubensteins had ended so badly, I was a little surprised when I saw them return. Frank had been angry and Ruth was scared—a classic tag team of denial. I suspect that they went to other doctors with the hope of finding a different answer. That's common enough: I'd probably do the same. Perhaps they simply decided not to deal with it at all. But burying your head in the sand only works for so long. After about a year, they returned to my office and became regulars.

For a while, their visits to the clinic were positive. With each subsequent appointment, the couple seemed to accept Ruth's diagnosis and did their best to deal with it. Then Ruth began to lose many of the social graces that masked her memory impairment. Embarrassed by her worsening power of recall, she withdrew from her friends. As a result, she became depressed. Medications for depression helped briefly, but did not curb the persistent progression of her cognitive decline. In time, Ruth struggled to keep up with her household chores. She burned meals repeatedly and forgot simple recipes. Her husband compensated by ordering out or buying prepared meals from the grocery store. When she could no longer clean, he hired a maid.

Despite her decline, it was a loving relationship, the kind we could all hope for. Frank's patience with Ruth was magnificent, a sign of a deep love that had grown over the years. When she forgot a name or a memory, he gently redirected her. He doted on her constantly, offering her a hand when she got up from a chair or his arm when they walked down the hallway. One day, about a year after they began seeing me, Frank pulled me aside as they were leaving my office. Like a young teen sheepishly buying condoms for the first time, he asked me if I had any samples for something that might help his impotence. Their love life had never been better, he explained, and he was having trouble meeting Ruth's daily sexual demands—not uncommon for a married couple when one of them has dementia. I left the office that day smiling to myself. We all like to believe that our parents and grandparents never have sex, that it's an activity reserved for the young and vibrant. Funny how little we know (or want to know).

Over time, Ruth's mental decline continued and Frank was increasingly unable to compensate for his added responsibilities in her daily care. During doctor's appointments he too appeared increasingly tired and unkempt. It was clear that taking care of his wife had become a round-the-clock job. The strain was taking its toll. Given his own decline, I gently began to suggest that Frank consider hiring full-time help or place his wife in a nursing home. I could have predicted the response.

"How dare you suggest that I put my wife in a nursing home? Does it look like I can't take care of her?" I bit my tongue and asked him to consider hiring an aide to assist him so he could leave the house from time to time. This suggestion didn't fare much better.

"Why can't Medicare pay for that? How much money do you think I have?"

Sadly, I told him that the federal health care system would not pay for custodial care of his wife but that the assistance might help keep her out of a more expensive nursing home. Then he was beside himself. "Why the hell did I pay all that money into Medicare over the years when they don't pay for anything?"

He was preaching to the choir—but it didn't change anything.

Despite the obvious financial strain, a few weeks later, Frank finally did hire an aide. Unfortunately, the additional assistance didn't help for long. Almost three years to the day after the couple had first walked into my office, I received a call from the emergency room. Ruth had pneumonia and would need to be hospitalized. Initially, she was started on antibiotics and began to improve. On the second evening of her hospital stay, however, she became extremely confused. Not knowing where she was, she got out of bed in the middle of the night and became tangled in her IV tubing. She began to walk across the hospital room and fell awkwardly to the floor. Sometime later, she was found on the floor by a nurse's aide. X-rays followed, revealing that she had broken her hip and would require surgery.

Things quickly went from bad to worse. During recovery following surgery, Ruth suffered a pulmonary embolus and became even less stable. Her blood pressure became tenuous and her breathing became labored. As she became increasingly short of breath, I sat with Frank, asking him to consider options for her care. I told him that if things continued, she would require a tube to help her breathe, something she had once told me in the office that she would not want. I suggested to him that it was okay to consider letting her go. We would take care of her and ensure that she did not die in pain.

My entreaties fell on deaf ears.

A tube was placed down her throat to help her breathe and she was transferred to an intensive care unit. Several weeks later, she finally did improve, vindicating Frank's staunch support. Nevertheless, Ruth had been left weak to the point where she could no longer get out of bed, let alone walk. After discussions with her husband, she was transferred to Steere House.

RUTH WAS ASLEEP IN BED, quietly snoring, when I entered her room a few minutes after my latest run-in with Frank. He was in the recliner beside her, his own eyes closed. Evidently, the bravado displayed at the front desk had taken a toll. I pulled up a chair between them and sat down. Under other circumstances, I might have left them alone to their dream worlds, but Frank's sense of urgency notwithstanding, we had several important issues to discuss. I gently nudged him and he startled for a second before opening a single eye. He grumbled something under his breath before sitting up.

"So, what's going on, Mr. Rubenstein?" I asked.

"Look at her, Dr. Dosa. She's skin and bone. I come in here every day at lunchtime to feed her so I can make sure she eats her meal. Lately, I can't get her to eat anything anymore."

He pointed to a mostly uneaten grilled cheese sandwich on a lunch tray in the corner of the room. A container of applesauce also appeared untouched.

"Mr. Rubenstein, your wife might be losing weight now because of her dementia."

"Doctor, if you are here to ask me to consider putting my wife on hospice again, I don't want to hear it. We've been down that road before."

"This isn't about whether or not your wife belongs on hospice."

He stared at me with a quiet determination. He was the defender at the gates of her castle and I was the leader of the invading horde. There would be no agreement or compromise. I knew that and for the time being, that was all right. Ruth probably wasn't ready for hospice, but there was another pressing issue to discuss. Did it make sense to order a number of tests and procedures to determine why she was losing weight?

I tried a different tack.

"Frank, how do you think your wife is doing?" I asked.

The question surprised him. He was expecting another assault on his castle gates.

"Dr. Dosa, I know my wife has a terrible disease, but I'm not ready to give up on her. She still loves me and my time with her is important."

I considered my next statement carefully.

"I know you care deeply about your wife, but I should tell you what I think. You talked with Mary earlier about wanting Ruth to see a gastroenterologist for her weight loss. I don't think sending her to a specialist is going to change anything. She's just going to end up getting a bunch of tests. Some of those tests have the potential to be quite uncomfortable. Besides, even if those tests show that she has cancer, Frank, you know as well as I do that we wouldn't consider doing anything aggressive. She wouldn't tolerate it."

The anger returned to Frank's face. I had stepped over the line and he responded accordingly.

"Doctor, I want you to do everything for my wife that you would want for your wife or your own children. If her heart stops, I want you to restart it. If she gets that pneumonia again, I want you to send her to the hospital. If she needs a specialist, I want you to send her. Am I being clear?"

"Crystal clear, Mr. Rubenstein."

I got up to leave the room and made my way to the door. When I got to the threshold, I looked back at him and his sleeping wife. Against my better judgment, I left Frank with one last parting thought.

"Frank, I know you love your wife."

He looked up at me and I could see the anger draining from his face.

I paused for a moment. I didn't know how far I could take it.

"Sometimes, the deepest act of love is letting go," I said. "Don't make this about fighting with me or any of the other staff. Think about Ruth."

I FOUND MARY WAITING when I returned to the front desk. Oscar had also returned to his more exposed position and was once again asleep.

"How did it go?" she asked.

"Status quo," I replied.

Mary shook her head.

"I'll call the GI doctor tomorrow and make an appointment," she said. She knew what Frank was after and had been hoping that I could dissuade him. She walked into her office to write herself a reminder.

"It's not going to make a difference, is it?" I could hear her just fine through the open door.

"No, Mary, it isn't, but he's not ready to hear that."

"Give him time," she said.

"We've got plenty of that."

CHAPTER SEVEN

"I have studied many philosophers and many cats.
The wisdom of cats is infinitely superior."

HIPPOLYTE TAINE

IT WAS JUST AN ORDINARY WEDNESDAY. OR SO I thought until I encountered a new face working behind the third floor nurse's desk. Actually, it was an old face and it belonged to a woman whom I guessed to be in her early eighties. She was tastefully dressed in a light blue cashmere sweater with carefully applied makeup and meticulously painted nails. Her graying golden hair was pulled back behind her ears and arranged with an expensive-looking antique clasp.

Mary spoke before I could say anything. "Dr. Dosa, I'd like to introduce you to Louise Chambers. She's our new receptionist."

"Our what?" The third floor didn't have a receptionist; it wasn't in the budget. Mary laughed at my confusion. "Just one of the patients, David."

I noticed that Louise was picking up the phone when it hadn't rung and saying something into the mouthpiece. I recalled another patient Mary had told me about, a former insurance salesman who sat in his room with his feet on a desk, selling insurance into a disconnected phone.

"Is she new?" I asked.

"Oh, no, not at all. Louise has been here for about three months. Lately, though, she's started to wander down to the front desk and sit here with us. Sometimes, if we're not around, she'll answer the phone."

I looked at Louise, who was repeatedly lifting up the phone and putting it back down again, and wondered how many family members had tried to get through while she had been manning the front desk.

"Look, I know finances are tight and you could use the help," I began.

"C'mon, David," Mary laughed, "lighten up. The families just love her. I think she was a secretary for some big executive years ago. Answering phones is probably just in her blood." She glanced over at Louise, who seemed to be watching us out of the corner of her eye. "And you know, David, she just *loves* tall men."

At this Louise muttered something, which prompted a childish laugh from Mary.

"What did she say?" I asked, moving toward the desk.

"I told you she would like you," Mary replied.

"But what did she say?"

"She says you're cute."

I shook my head incredulously.

"How did you get that?"

"Years of working here, I guess."

I had noted this Dr. Dolittle–like ability of Mary's before. She could understand patients no one else could—just one of her many talents.

Mary got up from her desk and grabbed a chart from the rack behind her.

"Take a look at this," Mary said. "It's Saul Strahan's labs."

The antibiotics I had prescribed for his leg didn't seem to be helping, and there were other complications. His white count appeared to bear the signs of worsening infection and he was likely dehydrated based on his recent labs.

"I'll go see him," I said.

Mary nodded, but not in a manner that conveyed much hope.

"I think we both know which way this is going," she said. "Now if only we could bring his daughter inside the tent."

That was a big tent she was talking about but in my experience, you couldn't get people inside until they were good and ready. Saul's daughter was a long way from ready.

"Well, let me go take a look at him," I said, and headed off for his room. As I passed Louise she got up quickly from her chair and stepped in front of me. Her hands opened wide, as if expecting a hug.

"You see," said Mary, "she really *does* like you."

I gave Louise a hug, which prompted a huge smile on her face.

Suddenly I understood.

"She thinks I'm somebody else!" I backed off a bit, feeling slightly offended. I headed for Saul's room with Mary laughing behind me.

"You know, David, whoever you're substituting for, you're not half bad."

• • •

I FOUND SAUL in his recliner again. The TV was on but he made no pretense of watching it. He was still wearing his Red Sox cap. Like so many others in this part of New England, Saul was a devoted sports fan. His room was festooned with baseball paraphernalia and mementoes. On his nightstand there was a picture of him standing proudly in front of Fenway Park with his arm around the neck of a young boy, likely his grandson.

"Spring training starts soon, Saul!" I said and pulled up a chair beside him. I wondered if he even knew his team had finally won the World Series. Even Sox fans that hadn't suffered strokes couldn't quite believe that the eighty-six-year-old Curse of the Bambino had finally ended.

I listened to Saul's heart and lungs and then finished my assessment by looking at his leg. Mary was right: It was inflamed again, despite the earlier antibiotic treatment. This time, though, the redness appeared to be spreading up his leg toward his knee. I took a moment to draw a line around the redness with a ballpoint pen—a line of demarcation to tell whether the infection would respond to our treatments. Then I sat down next to Saul and surveyed his other labs, quickly noticing a recent test that showed he was colonized with an increasingly common, highly resistant bacterium. This particularly nasty strain of staphylococcus has become the bane of every physician's existence in recent years. These resistant strains of bacteria have become almost ubiquitous in health care institutions around the world.

As I pondered my limited treatment options, I felt another presence in the room. I looked down to see Oscar sitting on the floor, watching me intently.

"Hey, you. Are you making rounds with me now?"

I reached over and offered my hand. Oscar sniffed it intently, then stood up to move toward me, allowing me to gently scratch him behind the ears. Then with a single leap, he jumped on my lap and sat down, eyeing me. He purred.

"So, what do you think?" I asked Oscar, nodding my head toward the patient.

For a second, he looked over at Saul as if he were actually assessing the situation. Then he jumped off my lap and approached the chair. He leaped up on the arm of the recliner and sniffed the air. Then he jumped down and scampered out of the room. It occurred to me that I had just received a second opinion from a cat.

I finished my exam and said good-bye to Saul. Returning to the front desk, I found Mary busy writing in a chart.

"So, I've just been on rounds with Oscar," I announced, smiling.

"Are you a believer now?" she asked.

"I wouldn't go that far but I've been wondering. Let's say, for the sake of argument, that he has this ability to sense when death is coming. Do you think he just smells a hormone or something you or I can't perceive?"

"I don't know, David. I'd like to think it's a little more than that, but I've read about stories from health care workers who say they can smell when death is near."

I considered what Mary was saying and realized that there was at least one possible scientific explanation.

"When cells stop working, you get a state of starvation and you can smell ketones," I said, referring to the sweet-smelling chemical by-product that can also be sensed in out-of-control diabetics.

Mary shrugged. "Personally, I'd like to believe that there's more here than just a smell. Maybe Oscar's patterning the behavior of the staff on the floor. After all, you were in the room just now showing interest in Saul. Perhaps he just wanted to be part of the team? A cat's got to earn his keep, you know."

I looked down the hallway, lost in thought. "In a way that makes sense," I said, "but it doesn't explain why he's sometimes the first to enter a room when a patient is dying."

I must have been frowning because Mary punched me in the arm in a playful fashion. "Careful!" she said. "You look like you might hurt yourself!"

"It's funny," I said. "I've had all of this medical education and experience and I still often walk into a room and have no idea what is going to happen. I mean, how often do family members ask you how long their loved one has?"

"All the time."

"What do you tell them?"

"I tell them that only God really knows and I don't have his telephone number."

"Like a cat," I said, unconsciously.

"*What?*" Now Mary was the one who looked incredulous.

"You know: 'A dog comes when you call and a cat takes a message and gets back to you.'" I looked under the desk where the cats' food was kept: no Oscar. "The thing is, Oscar walked into the room just now, took a deep whiff, and walked out of there as if there was nothing to worry about."

"I guess he knows that you're going to fix Mr. Strahan."

"Maybe. But it does bring you down a peg, knowing that in the great medical org chart, you're in a box below a cat."

Mary chuckled at my response. As I looked at her, I suddenly became curious about her own thoughts related to our cat.

"Mary, when did you first think about what Oscar was doing?"

She put her pen down and sat back in her chair.

"I guess, at first, I didn't really think about it. Some of the aides started to talk about the cat always being there when patients died. As I remember it, I suspect Oscar's first patient was Marion McCullough. Her son Jack used to bring Oscar into the room with him because her mother really loved cats. Oscar would never really stay with her for long, but as she got sicker, he would stay longer. On the day Marion died, Oscar actually jumped into her bed of his own accord and sat down beside her. Jack telephoned me a few days later and told me how fortunate it had been that Oscar jumped on the bed."

"Why?"

"I guess he thought it was a signal that she was going to die soon."

Mary looked over at me.

"At the time, I thought it was a cute story, but I didn't give it much thought. You should talk to him, though."

"So, that was your first inkling," I said. "But what did it for you?"

"I suppose the thing that made me a believer was a death that occurred several months later. By then, a number of people were talking about Oscar, including several of the hospice nurses. Your patient Ralph Reynolds was dying and we were trying to do everything to make him more comfortable. One of your colleagues was up here and went in to take a look at him. She came out suggesting that he was close to death and gave some hospice recommendations. One of the aides overheard her and went off to find Oscar."

Mary paused for a second, savoring the telling. "The aide returned a few minutes later, carrying one unhappy kitty into the room. She put Oscar on the bed and announced to us that if the patient were dying, Oscar should be present. Oscar looked at all of us like we were all stark mad and ran out of the room quicker than she could finish her sentence. Hours later, we found him hiding under the nurse's desk."

"So, what happened?"

"Ralph actually hung on for another thirty-six hours. But sure enough, four hours before he died, we found Oscar pacing in front of the patient's closed door. Oscar looked profoundly unhappy. When we opened the door, he dashed straight for the bed and leaped up next to Ralph. He curled up there and refused to budge. A few hours later, Ralph was gone. Oscar didn't leave his side until the funeral director came and even then, we needed to bribe him with cat treats to get him away from Ralph."

I shook my head, but I don't know if it was in wonder or disbelief. Mary gauged my reaction and offered me a hint of a smile.

"Dr. Dosa, it looks like you're starting to take our cat here more seriously."

I threw up my hands. "Who knows, Mary? I'm still a scientist at heart." I knew Mary hated my *I'm a scientist* talk, but I continued. "I've always been taught to look dispassionately at the facts—to analyze them, form theories, and then poke holes in them until other theories develop that are closer to the truth. You know that. When you consider it from a scientific point of view it's easy to shrug off suggestions that a cat can predict death. It's so much easier to say that he's just sitting with those patients because of the activity—the gathering of family, the holding of hands, the saying of good-byes. It just makes more sense. Or maybe he just likes to hang out with dying people because they don't bother him. Most cats sleep two thirds of the day anyway, so chances are a cat is going to be found on a warm bed somewhere, right?"

Mary smiled widely. She seemed to sense that I had reached some sort of tipping point and that I was prepared to believe in this gift of Oscar's. She didn't want to push it, but she couldn't seem to help herself either. "But you've got to admit that there's something unusual about our cat, right?"

"When you consider all the circumstantial evidence, it certainly looks that way."

"So, do some more investigating," she said reasonably. "You're a researcher. I think you should talk to some of the family members of the patients who died on Oscar's watch, see what they have to say."

"I guess it couldn't hurt," I said. I was thinking about the part of my job that required me to be a detective. Science is, among other things, an art of detection. I felt that I had to get closer to the heart of this mystery.

"So, where should I begin?" I asked.

"I'd start with someone you trust," Mary prompted.

"Donna Richard?" I asked.

"I can't think of anyone better!" she said, perhaps a little more self-satisfied than was necessary.

I hate it when she's right.

CHAPTER EIGHT

"Cats always know whether people like or dislike them. They do not always care enough to do anything about it."

WINIFRED CARRIERE

TO SAY THAT I TRUSTED DONNA RICHARD WAS SOMEthing of an understatement. It was like saying that Sherlock Holmes trusted Dr. Watson, or that Captain Kirk trusted Scotty to run the engine room.

As any doctor will tell you, good office managers are worth their weight in gold. They manage large staffs, stay one step ahead of government regulations, and make sure that important phone calls get returned. They see that the billing is current and that everyone gets paid, and make sure we don't run out of supplies—everything from tongue depressors to copier paper. Office manager is one of those thankless jobs that only gets noticed when something goes wrong. That may be why it can be such a difficult position to fill. I know that's why we snapped up Donna Richard when she, quite literally, landed on our doorstep.

Donna had brought her mother into our office one morning for an appointment and happened to ask one of my colleagues if we needed an office manager. She had recently returned to Rhode Island after fifteen years in California to take care of her parents and needed a job. Talk about synchronicity.

During the three years we worked together, Donna and I would often chat long after my patients and the rest of the staff had gone home. We would sit together in my office as we finished up paperwork. She'd ask me about my newborn son, offering the kind of parenting advice you couldn't find in any medical manual. In turn, I'd ask her about the balancing act she performed every day as a single working mother with the added responsibilities of caring for a parent with dementia. It was during those evening talks that I first saw the complexities of dementia care through the eyes of a friend. Donna opened up to me about the compromises she made in leaving her career to return home to take care of her mother. She spoke of the difficulties of navigating the health care system—one that she knew well from her days as a senior health care executive—to ensure that her mother had high-quality care. It was Donna who introduced me to the term "sandwich generation," and it was from her that I began to really understand what it's like for the millions of Americans caught between raising kids and caring for elderly family.

Now I hoped she could help me once more by giving me some much-needed perspective on Oscar. But first we had to catch up. It had been two years since Donna left our office for another job and over a year since her mother had passed away with Oscar by her side. We had a lot of ground to cover.

"IN THE WEEKS AFTER my mother died I would wake up in a cold sweat." I was sitting with Donna in her suburban home outside of Providence. "My mother would come to me in my dreams," she continued. "She was younger, the way I remember her from my childhood, and she would look up at and accuse me: 'I wanted to go to the hospital but you didn't let me . . . . If you had just sent me to the hospital.'"

Donna looked up at a far-off corner of the ceiling, as if the movement itself would keep her from crying. She took a drag off her cigarette and let the smoke waft up through the air.

"David, I know how much you hate my smoking," she said with a smile.

I rolled my eyes but said nothing. It's not my place to come into someone's home and tell them to stop smoking. I do that enough in the office.

Donna considered the cigarette again and then stamped it out in the ashtray. "After one of those dreams I would sit in bed for hours, trying to talk myself out of what she had said. I knew she didn't like the nursing home, or at least she didn't like it when she could still process things. You have to realize, putting her in the home was the hardest decision of my life, but I really had no other choice. I was a single mom trying to provide for my son as best I could. I just couldn't take care of her at home anymore. She had that dementia with Lewy bodies and her decline was just so quick."

Aside from neurologists, geriatricians, and psychiatrists, few people are familiar with Lewy body dementia (LBD). Though it's likely the second most common cause of dementia, LBD is frequently underdiagnosed because of its similarities to Parkinson's and Alzheimer's diseases. As with Parkinson's, LBD involves a movement disorder: Those afflicted become rigid and unsteady on their feet. They frequently suffer from psychotic symptoms such as hallucinations, sleep disturbances, and significant behavioral changes—as well as an extreme sensitivity and intolerance to the antipsychotic medications that are often mistakenly prescribed for the hallucinations. This behavioral component of the disease makes caring for patients with LBD especially difficult.

"It was like one minute, my mother was fine, and the next month she was lost. She just wasn't herself anymore. We took her to the best doctors, the best specialists, and they would give her pill after pill. She must have tried them all at one point. The doctors thought she was depressed, so they gave her antidepressants. She couldn't sleep, so they gave her sleeping pills. Her memory failed, so they gave her a memory pill. The more medications they gave her, the worse she got. Eventually, things got so out of hand that your colleague finally admitted her to a psychiatric hospital just to wean her off the medications. Turns out, they probably were just making it worse."

She shook her head at the irony of it all. "Kind of strange that we had to admit her to a hospital to get her *off* medications."

It's actually not so strange. Over one-quarter of hospitalizations today result from the collective effects of overmedication. The fact is that all medications, even herbal and over-the-counter drugs, are potentially dangerous in certain clinical situations. Elderly patients today are exposed to more and more medications all the time.

"When she got out of the hospital," Donna continued, "it was obvious that she couldn't come home. From that point on she went from one nursing home to another. What an eye-opener that was!

"When my mother was in the first nursing home, I got a phone call from the nurse at the facility telling me they were sending her to the emergency room for evaluation. I asked them why and she told me that, at eighty-four years of age, my mother had hit an aide while they were trying to change her. Now, my mom was feisty, but she never would have done this if it wasn't for her disease. I rushed off to the ER and they did the workup. The doctors ended up finding nothing, but when they tried to get her back to the facility, the nursing home refused to take her. In the end, my mother stayed in the emergency room for three days while we tried to find a place for her to go."

Donna got up from her chair and walked nervously around her kitchen.

"You know, David, this is what really gets me. It was like no one in the hospital really cared where my mother ended up. They just wanted to get her out of the ER as soon as possible. I had to fight tooth and nail; finally, I was able to pull strings and get my mother into a nursing home like Steere House. To this day, I know that the only reason they took my mother was because I knew all of the doctors who worked there. Imagine if I hadn't had those connections or hadn't known how to find information about those different nursing homes? The whole system is just plain bad."

Donna became quiet. The memories washed over her and again tears came to her eyes. This time she let them flow.

"Sometimes, when I think about those days, I don't know how I did it. I had a plan every day that was minute-to-minute; I had to have a strategy just to be able to work, care for my son, and be there for my mother."

"That must have been hard on you."

Donna looked at me as if I'd just said something like "It must snow a lot in New England in the winter."

"David, unless you go through it, you truly have no idea. I had no life for myself."

In anyone else this might have seemed like self-pity. With Donna it was just the facts.

"I had no life, but that wasn't so bad. I could deal with that. I understood that this was my cross to bear. The worst part was the guilt about not being there for someone else. When I would miss my son's swimming meet because something was going on with my mom, I would feel terrible. When I would go to the swimming meet, I would feel guilty that I was not visiting my mother. Sometimes when I left Steere House, I would feel so guilty about putting my mother in the nursing home that I would drive home crying the whole way. 'Good Italians' are not supposed to put their parents into nursing homes."

Donna managed a halfhearted smile and shrugged her shoulders.

"In the end, I guess I didn't have a choice. I just did the best I could."

She looked at me and I could tell that we had gone as far as she intended to go.

"Doesn't stop the guilt, though?" I asked.

"It never really goes away. And those dreams . . ."

WE TALKED for another two hours, about everything from her job to her social life as a single parent, and then I told her about the recent birth of my daughter. Eventually I glanced at my watch and realized how late it had become. I got up off the kitchen stool and began to gather my things.

"Wait!" Donna said. She looked at me with the hint of a smile. "You came here wanting to find out about Oscar and you almost left without asking me."

"I guess our conversation seemed to go in a different direction," I said. "Or maybe I'm not as open to the idea of Oscar as I thought I was."

She laughed and gestured for me to sit down again.

"So, Ms. Richard," I said, putting on my best reporter's voice, "what do you think about our four-legged friend, Oscar?"

Donna laughed and gave me her *Oh brother!* look, an expression I hadn't seen since we worked together.

"First off, my mother hated cats! Earlier in her life, I would have half expected her to poison Oscar had he jumped on her bed. It wasn't just cats. My mother really didn't like animals, period. Didn't see the point of them. Yet, as she got worse and worse with the dementia, she seemed to take more comfort from the animals on the unit. I don't know what it was about them, or about the changes in my mother, but something really had changed. It was like she was more receptive on some deeper level. Does that sound strange?"

"Not at all. In fact, lately I've been wondering a lot about the true nature of our connection with animals, especially when we're very young and very old. My son has always been drawn to animals, even before he could talk. I've seen that same intense curiosity with some of my patients, too. It's as if the relationship somehow transcends language. I'm just now learning how smart animals are."

"Well, Oscar was smart. That much I'll say. He generally kept a safe distance and left my mother alone, but when he'd wander by and she would stop to talk to him, well, he stopped too. He never stayed long and he never cuddled up to her—Oscar was more like a visiting dignitary than a house cat—but he always stopped as if to hear her out."

Visiting dignitary indeed.

"What did you think of the animals at Steere House?"

"Well, in a way, it was strangely comforting. A distraction of sorts. I mean, it didn't change the fact that my mother was in the nursing home, but it did make her surroundings a little more bearable. More like *home* than *a home,* you know? In a way, I think the presence of the animals also helped my son."

"What do you mean?"

"Well, nursing homes are not easy places for kids. Sometimes he'd come up to the floor and go off in search of the cats. It was better for him, playing with Billy or Munchie on the first floor rather than sitting in a straight-backed chair swinging his legs. And it would give me a little more time to spend with my mother."

"Was Oscar there at the end?"

"Absolutely. When my mother got sick for the last time, Oscar spent more and more time in the room with me. It was as if he knew I needed the support. It was truly bizarre. He seemed to warm toward me. More than that . . . he seemed to understand."

Donna gauged the look on my face and continued.

"Well, I was at the bedside for pretty much the last seventy-two hours of my mother's life. I even slept in the recliner next to her during that time. When I would try to rest, Oscar would wander into the room and snuggle up next to me. Then he would jump over from my chair to my mother's bed and sit down beside her. He did that for pretty much the entire time that my mother was dying.

"The thing I can't get over is that Oscar always seemed to know when he was needed, and he never seemed to want anything in return. Oh, he'd let me stroke under his chin and rub his little ears, but even that—well, it was as if he knew that it was helping me. Which it did. There's something really calming about petting a cat . . ."

"Was he there when she died?"

"A few hours before my mother died, one of the nurses came to talk with me and convinced me to go home for a little bit. I wasn't sure if it was a good idea, but the nurse persuaded me to go. Sure enough, my mother died shortly after I left. Oscar never left, though. He was there when she drew her last breath."

"Were you upset that you left before she died?"

"No. Quite honestly, my mother probably waited for me to leave before she let go. That was just her style."

Donna smiled.

"Besides," she said, "she wasn't alone. My mother had Oscar."

CHAPTER NINE

"A cat is a puzzle for which there is no solution."

HAZEL NICHOLSON

IT WAS AS IF I HAD STUMBLED ON A SCENE FROM THE Summer of Love. A small group of interested onlookers, residents, and staff had surrounded the front desk of the unit, blocking my view of the spectacle. Like a small child trying to get a better look at a passing parade, I picked my way through the morass of walkers and residents. All eyes were on Oscar and Maya, who appeared to be in the throes of ecstasy. Both cats were charging around the desk at breakneck speed, stopping occasionally to roll around, flailing their limbs in the air. It was like watching a drug-fueled pas de deux, with cats instead of dancers.

I pushed my way to the front, where I found Mary.

"Who put the Benzedrine in Mrs. Murphy's Ovaltine?" I said.

"Catnip," she said.

Watching their whirling-dervish routine, my inner veterinarian took over. "Are they sick?" I asked.

Mary laughed, and then launched into an explanation, almost shouting to be heard over the yowling of the cats and the laughter of the staff and patients.

"Cats love it—it makes them crazy. There's some kind of chemical in the herb that gives them an almost sexual high."

I looked at Oscar, whom I had been thinking of as this wise, Sphinx-like creature with all the answers. He was chasing his tail. "What, do they smoke it?"

"Don't you know anything about cats?" asked an aide who overheard me. I was joking but honestly, I had little idea what catnip was.

"I've never owned a cat," I said to the aide.

She laughed. "Nobody owns a cat, Dr. Dosa. They own you!"

Mary came to my rescue.

"The cats don't smoke it, David," she said. "They just roll in it. You can see the results."

"But they do act like little drug fiends!" said the aide.

As the hilarity died down, the novelty of seeing our two resident cats acting like clowns wore off even before the catnip did. People began to drift off and I stole into Mary's office to check my messages. She followed me in.

"How was your meeting with Donna?" she asked.

"Interesting," I said. "She told me that her mother really hated cats, all animals really, until she met Oscar."

"Isn't that something?" said Mary. "That you could even forget what you once hated."

"An old Irish patient of mine asked me if I knew the definition of Irish Alzheimer's," I said.

Mary cocked an eyebrow, waiting for the joke. "And?"

"He said, 'You forget everything but the grudges.'"

Mary laughed. "Well, I don't think the Irish have a lock on resentment." She looked out the window at the thinning crowd. Oscar and Maya were lolling about on the floor now, a couple of old hopheads coming down off their high.

"But Donna also told me how glad *she* was that Oscar was there at the end," I continued. "It was as if he gave her permission to leave. She said later she figured her mother wasn't going to die with her daughter there, so Oscar did a service for both of them, in a sense."

"Like a bridge between the mother and daughter," Mary said.

"Yeah, like a bridge." I looked through the glass with her at this ordinary house cat, passed out on the carpet. Maybe I was the one who'd been smoking the catnip.

"So, are you going to talk to some more family members?" Mary asked. "Remember those two sisters who lost both their parents here? Oscar was with their mom when she died."

"Rita and Annette," I said. "I thought about them. Though I'm not really sure what I'm trying to discover." I looked at her again.

"You could always go see Jack McCullough . . . or what about Mrs. Ferretti? Didn't you have a good relationship with her?"

I could sense Mary prodding me on with my journey of discovery. "Did you ever see *Citizen Kane*?" I asked.

"Oh, God, ages ago."

"Maybe I'm like that reporter, you know, the one who goes out to discover the meaning of 'Rosebud.' "

"That's right!" said Mary. "And in the end it turns out to be the name of his sled."

"Yeah, that's what the audience finds out when they show them burning it at the end," I said. "But the reporter never learns anything."

"You never know, though, until you try."

I smiled and changed the subject, "So, who do I need to see today?"

YOU KNOW WHAT THEY SAY about the weather in New England? "If you don't like it now just wait a few minutes." My day at Steere House turned out to be just as fickle as our climate. Less than an hour after the hilarity of the crazy-cat carousel, no one was laughing. In fact, the atmosphere had become toxic.

Just an hour or so before everyone had been laughing as if they were at the circus. Now it seemed I had stepped right into the midst of a heated battle between Mary and a well-dressed, middle-aged woman I recognized to be Saul Strahan's daughter, Barbara. Two nursing aides were standing silently beside the desk, watching the two of them go at it, apparently over a pair of slippers.

Mary was trying to placate Barbara Strahan. "I appreciate this may be upsetting, but if we can keep this in perspective . . ."

"Don't you tell me about perspective! I don't need—" and before I could slip past she recognized me as her father's doctor.

"Can't you do anything about your staff up here?" she said to me. "This is the third pair of slippers that they've lost in the last two years."

Finding myself in the middle of a conflict I knew nothing about, I said nothing. Barbara threw up her hands, then turned her fury back to Mary and the aides.

"Is it too much to ask that you keep track of my father's stuff?"

Mary offered a cautious explanation.

"I'm sure that your father's slippers will show up soon. One of the other residents probably just took them from his closet. We'll find them eventually. We almost always do."

"Why can't you keep the other patients out of my father's room?"

"We try, Barbara, it's just that it's very hard to control what they get into when we're not watching."

"Well, try harder!"

As if to emphasize her point, Barbara made eye contact with each of us one by one, and then stormed off. But before she did, she took one last look at Lydia, a Spanish-speaking aide.

"You guys need to get better help around here," she said. "Or at least someone who speaks better English!"

With that parting shot, she stormed off down the hallway toward her father's room.

I looked over at Lydia. A tear had come to her eye, one that she quickly wiped off with the back of her hand.

Mary put her hand on Lydia's shoulder.

"She doesn't mean it," she said. "She's just upset."

Lydia nodded and attempted a smile, but the insult had stung deep and I could tell that it would take some time for her to recover. She turned and walked away. The rest of us remained in awkward silence. Mary shook her head and then turned to an aide.

"See if you can find those slippers," she said quietly.

"Well, as always, I timed my arrival perfectly," I said as the young woman left. "What was that all about?"

"*That* was Saul Strahan's daughter. I thought you two had met."

"Only once, when her father was admitted. Mostly we just talk on the phone. We've been talking a lot lately."

I sat down at the desk and looked directly at Mary. A perfectionist in her work, she was probably seething inside. Aside from her own pride, injured by the accusation that she didn't run a tight ship, I knew that she felt even worse for the aides.

"I need to go outside for a cigarette," Mary said. She walked back into the nurse's office and spent several minutes searching for her pack. When she emerged without her coat, I could tell that she had already calmed down.

"Seriously, Mary, doesn't that get on your nerves?"

She sighed. "It's hard to believe sometimes, but I've worked here for almost ten years, and at a lot of other nursing homes before that. At this point in my career, I can pretty much put every family member I meet into one of four categories: those who are angry, those who feel guilty, those who are afraid, and those who are all three. We try to work with everyone to eventually accept *this*," she said, holding up her hands to encompass the ward, the residents, and the finality of it all. "In time, most of them do. Sometimes we just can't get them to accept this reality quickly enough."

"So, what is Barbara Strahan?" I asked. "Which category does she fall into?"

"She probably just feels guilty."

Mary paused to consider what to say.

"You know, David, Saul probably hasn't worn those slippers in the last half year anyway. But if I don't find them immediately, she'll be speaking with my boss."

"Have you tried talking with her?"

"In one ear, out the other."

"Sometimes, I don't know how you do it," I said. "At least, as physicians, we get to come and go."

"Actually, the ones who feel guilty, like Barbara, are easier to deal with than some of the others. You just have to develop a thick skin. They usually just yell at us about silly things and most of them calm down eventually. Barbara will probably even come down here and apologize for her behavior before she leaves. Some of the other family members can be worse."

"Worse?"

"Well, as I said, there are families who are afraid of the disease and what it does. I get it. But they're usually the ones who are the most in denial. They'll come in here and question everything. If we change a resident's diet, they'll ask a million questions about why. Those cases end up being harder because you feel so sorry for the family. When they finally get it, what's actually happening to their mother or father, they look like they've been beaten with a two-by-four."

Mary sighed again.

"I'm sorry that you can't smoke in here," I said.

"No, you're not," she said, and smiled. "Finally, there are the angry ones who blame us for everything. Just last week, I had a daughter ask me why her mother was in one of those walkers. When I told her it was because she had fallen down a couple of times, she said that I didn't want her mother to get better! 'You probably want her out of here so you can have her bed,' she said."

"You're kidding!"

"I wish."

I understand how hard it is to see a loved one fail the way so many of these patients do. Quite frankly, I have no idea how I'd handle taking care of a parent or spouse with dementia. Maybe I'd be the same, casting about and blaming everyone, but from the outside looking in, I'm always perplexed at how some people accuse those who are merely trying to help. Our conversation was interrupted as Louise came wandering toward the front desk pushing her own walker. Mary noticed her first. "Your fan club has arrived," she said.

I got up from the desk and walked around to greet Louise. A hearty smile came to her face before she spoke.

"She says, 'You're so tall,'" Mary translated behind me.

I gave Louise a quick hug and she giggled. Then she wandered back down the hallway.

"She gets around pretty well," I said as she left.

"Mobility is not *her* problem," Mary replied. "She's always visiting the other patients, whether they know it or not."

Suddenly, Mary jumped up and raced down the hallway. She caught Louise a few doors down and rifled through the basket on the front of her walker. A few moments later, Mary returned to the desk carrying an assortment of articles.

She presented me with a beige sweater, a doctor's stethoscope—and a pair of men's slippers.

"Mrs. Chambers," she said, "our resident kleptomaniac."

She placed the stethoscope and sweater on the desk.

"This stethoscope belongs to a medical student who was up here working last week. I bet he's been looking everywhere for it."

She put it in her office for safekeeping and was about to take the slippers to Saul's room.

"Hold on," I said, before she could get past me. "Do you mind if I do the honors? I want to find out where her head is at."

Mary shrugged and handed me the pair of slippers. "Be my guest."

What I really wanted to do was give Saul's daughter a piece of my mind. It's not that I don't understand how hard it is to watch all of this happen to a loved one, but there are boundaries and Barbara had crossed several.

I found her lying on the bed, her head resting in her father's lap as my son's does sometimes when he's watching television. "I have the slippers," I said. Barbara lifted her head up and turned to face me. Her eyes were red, her mascara smeared. As she sat up, she wiped her eyes with the sleeve of her blouse.

I walked over and put the slippers on the bedside table. "You know," I said, "you were pretty hard on the staff out there."

She started to cry. Not a slow trickle of tears, but a soul-cleansing deluge.

Now I felt terrible for setting her off. As her tears slowed I grabbed a box of tissues off the table next to me and offered her one.

"Doctor, I'm so sorry for my behavior," she said as she dabbed at her eyes. "Can you tell Lydia that I'm sorry? I don't know what got into me. I feel like such a fool."

"You should probably tell her yourself. By the way, Lydia's one of our best aides. She goes to night school five times a week so she can improve her English."

She nodded. "It's just that I come in here and I don't know what to do," she said, pointing toward her father. "I can't even tell if he knows I'm here."

"You're doing everything you can for your father right now by just being here with him."

She nodded.

"My mind gets that," she said. "My heart doesn't."

It's a phrase I've heard a hundred times.

Intellectually, Barbara understood what had happened to her father, but when she looked at him, she could still only see the man who raised her.

"I mean, look at him. He just sits there with this stupid, vacant expression on his face."

I know she didn't mean it but her despair was driving the bus now.

"My father doesn't know who I am anymore," she continues. "This handsome man, who was everything to me growing up. He would walk me to school every day when I was little, and when I was older I could call him and talk about my problems at work, even boy trouble. Who am I to him now?"

"Ms. Strahan, is there anyone else you can talk with about all of this? These losses you're experiencing are enormous. No one should navigate them alone. Perhaps there's a support group, a therapist, or a minister?"

"I talk to my son sometimes, when he's around. It helps, I suppose."

A hint of a mother's smile came to her lips.

"You know, he's so good with him. He'll sit here and tell him jokes or read the sports pages to him. They used to go to Red Sox games together," she said, lifting her chin in the direction of the photo on the nightstand of Saul and a boy at Fenway that I had noticed before. "He doesn't get put off by any of . . . this place or his condition. Sometimes he can even get Dad to smile."

Barbara's expression changed once again to profound frustration. "But I can't do that!"

I nodded and sat with her in silence for a few moments. Sometimes doing my job means saying nothing at all.

"The thing is, Doctor," she finally said, "I feel so guilty all the time. Every time I leave here I cry all the way home."

She smiled through her tears. "I can't tell you how many blouses I've ruined with mascara stains. You'd think I'd know better by now."

Looking at her blouse, it became clear that another one would soon be relegated to the trash.

"Doctor, I know you think I'm wrong when I argue for more treatments for my dad." I started to speak but she held up her hand. "But you have to understand: Sometimes I feel that his medical wishes are the last thing of him I have left. He said he wanted everything done." She was crying again.

There was a longer conversation to be had about Saul's health and his end-of-life choices; it was one I'd had before with Barbara on the telephone and one I was sure we would have again, probably soon. But this was not the time. It was not time to say to her that the father who took her and her son to baseball games would never return.

"This isn't something you need to decide today," I said. "Though it won't make you feel any better, I understand how hard it is to see someone who still looks like your father, but has lost so much of what made him the person you knew. I've had caregivers who have lost family members to cancer and car accidents tell me it's far worse seeing someone close to them die slowly with dementia."

She nodded and I could see that she had accepted what I had just said. After a few moments of silence her tears ceased and her mood brightened. Maybe it was as simple as hearing that she wasn't alone in her grief.

"Thank you, Doctor."

"For the pair of slippers?" I replied, a grin coming to my face.

"Sure." She returned my smile. "For the slippers."

CHAPTER TEN

"A cat is always on the wrong side of the door."

ANONYMOUS

IT WAS TIME TO GET BACK ON THE TRAIL OF MY mystery—but where to turn? As usual, it was Mary who pointed me in the right direction.

"You know, David," she reminded me one afternoon while I was seeing patients, "you still haven't talked to Rita and Annette. Of all the families I've dealt with over the years, they've probably spent the most time at Steere House."

Of course.

The two sisters had spent an uninterrupted decade at the nursing home, tending first to their father, and then their mother. Who better to provide insight into my four-legged enigma?

I dialed Rita's number, figuring that they would never want to set foot inside a nursing home again. On the contrary, they offered to meet me at the nursing home a few days later.

"We're always happy to talk about Oscar," said Rita. "And it'll be nice to see our old friends as well."

As I drove to Steere House from a busy day at the outpatient clinic I couldn't help but think about the last decade of *my* life and everything that had changed. My own career had transitioned from medical school through three years of residency, two years of fellowship, and toward the development of an established medical career. I had met and married my wife and fathered two children—had gone from the sort of selfish, self-sufficient life of a bachelor to a family existence, with all its joys and responsibilities. Physically, I had changed too. Much to my displeasure, I had added twenty pounds to my frame, developed a receding hairline with more gray hair than I cared to have, and learned to cope with my own chronic illness and developing physical limitations.

It seemed slightly odd to me, if not unfair, that all that had occurred while Rita and Annette were caring for one parent after another—first at home and then at Steere House. As much as I like to tell my patients that dying is a part of living, it seemed like I had gotten the better end of the deal.

I found the sisters seated in the lobby, holding court with several of the nursing home's staff. It had been months since their almost daily visits, and it was clear that they were catching up with people who had become very important to them. I lingered in the background for a few moments, watching as aides and nurses came by to chat. I noticed how at ease each daughter was with the rest of the staff. There were no tears or sad faces, just laughter and warm smiles. It was a little like a family reunion, one I didn't want to interrupt. But Rita saw me hanging in the background and greeted me with a wave of her hand.

"Hello, Rita," I said. "You look well. You too, Annette."

We exchanged pleasantries as we walked toward the library.

"It must feel strange to be back," I offered.

Rita and Annette nodded but said nothing as we walked down the long corridor. They seemed lost in thought, as if each door they passed was a portal to a particular memory.

"A lot of people don't want to let go," Rita said, as if out of the blue. We were in the library now, and she seemed a little distracted, looking around a room that was part of her second home for years.

"Why do you think that is?" I asked. I knew from experience that letting go is precisely what family members struggle with the most, but I wanted Rita's take on it.

"Because you want them back in the worst possible way," she said. "You just want your parent back, the one who signed the report cards, the one who made the Thanksgiving dinner. But you can't."

Knowing that, and coming to terms with that knowledge, is really the most difficult part. A relationship between two people is made up, for the most part, of invisible things: memories, shared experiences, hopes, and fears. When one person disappears, the other is left alone, as if holding a string with no kite. Memories can do a lot to sustain you, but the invisible stuff of the relationship is lost, even as unresolved issues remain: arguments never settled, kind words never uttered, things left unsaid. They become like a splinter beneath the skin—unseen, but painful nevertheless. Until they're exposed, coping with the loss is impossible.

"So, how do you come to grips with the loss?" I asked.

Annette answered this time. "It takes time. But at first it's about diversion and misdirection."

I hadn't heard that before. "What do you mean?" I asked.

"I guess it's like this," Annette continued. "A few years after my father was diagnosed he called me late one night. I told him it was the middle of the night and he should go back to bed. But he was anxious."

"'There's a strange woman here with me,' he said. 'I want you to come over here and take me home.'"

Annette shook her head at the memory. "For almost an hour I stayed on the phone trying to convince him that the woman in his bed was my mother—his wife. Eventually I was able to convince him . . ."

"Dr. Dosa, it only got worse from there," Rita said.

"From that point on," Annette continued, "the phone calls started coming more frequently. I don't like to admit this to myself, but early on I think I got a little angry."

She paused and then broke into a smile. "Okay, a lot angry! I mean, how many times can you say that the *strange woman* is actually your mother? It was heartbreaking and frustrating at the same time. It was many things. But eventually you realize that the best way to cope with the repetitiveness is not through explanation but through distraction. I'd stop trying to convince my father that the strange woman was his wife and simply changed the subject to something else and then everything was okay."

"It was the same with our mother," Rita said. "When she became a resident on the third floor, she still recognized the nursing home as the place where she had come to see Dad before he died. It was one of the reasons she liked Steere House from the beginning: In her heart, she *knew* it—the layout, the rooms, the cats!"

Annette chimed in, "She really took to Maya. Oscar not so much," she laughed.

"And she still knew a lot of the staff, too, or at least they were familiar enough not to make her anxious. Sometimes we'd be sitting in her room and she would ask about my father." Rita smiled wryly. "We would tell her that our father was answering the telephone and would be back when he was done."

"Eventually you just become good at misdirection," Annette said. "I know I did."

"The little things you do," Rita said with a small laugh. They didn't sound so little to me.

"Did you ever feel guilty about—?"

"About lying?" Rita jumped in.

Annette shook her head emphatically. "We considered it playacting. You have to learn to play a role and distract a person with memory impairment." She smiled, then added, "We could never bring our mother back to our reality. We had to go to *hers.*"

"That helped us in a way, too," Rita said. "The distraction helped to keep us focused on the moment. Otherwise, well, your thoughts go forward and backward and don't have a place to settle. It can be unnerving."

Listening to them I realized that they had become, against their will, experts in the field.

"It sounds like you both really learned how to cope with the illness."

"Dr. Dosa, I don't want it to seem like it was easy," said Annette. "What worked for our father didn't work for our mother, so we needed to come up with different strategies. There were days when I would leave work in tears. I would have breakdowns."

Rita nodded in stoic agreement. "Toward the end, there were times when my mother couldn't tell who I was."

"So, how did you deal with that?" I asked.

"By taking comfort in the little things—"

This had a familiar ring to it.

"My mother liked Cajun music," Annette jumped in. "Even in the end, she would tap her foot to the beat of her favorite songs. Other times, even after she had stopped eating, it was ice cream. You do whatever makes them happy."

"Still, the nursing home does take some getting used to," Rita said. "For us as well as them."

I used her last statement as a segue into my questions regarding Oscar. "Did the fact that there were cats on the floor make it any easier to accept Steere House as a home for your parents?"

"Absolutely," Annette said. "Both my sister and I took great comfort in the fact that Oscar and Maya were here. It just makes the place so much more livable. They were such a nice distraction—not just for the residents, but for the visitors too. Watching a cat can be mesmerizing. You know the way a cat will find a sheath of light and just stretch out . . ."

"Kitty yoga!" Rita said. "And the way it will stare out of the window as if the Macy's parade is passing by? And what about the way it will clean itself as if nothing else matters in the world?"

You can say that again, I thought.

"The cats proved to be . . . well, another diversion. A lovely one at that," Rita said.

"Was Oscar there at the end for your mother?"

Rita smiled before she answered. "Dr. Dosa, if I hadn't been there, I wouldn't have believed it."

"Believed what?"

"There were several false alarms with my mother before she died. With every turn for the worse, Oscar would come in and out of the room, checking in on her. He wouldn't stay for long. Sometimes he would simply come in, smell her feet, and then leave again."

Smell her feet? That was a new one.

"Were you surprised?"

"No, we had heard that the cat did these things from other families on the unit."

Taking a deep breath, Rita launched into the story of her mother's last day.

"At first, it was just the distinct sounds of scratching—*scratch, scratch, scratch*. I remember looking at my sister, wondering where it was coming from. We looked out the door and didn't see any cat. Then it would come again: *scratch, scratch, scratch*. This went on for probably an hour before there was a knock on the door."

"Then one of the aides walks into the room," Annette interjected, "closing the door behind her. She asks if we would be okay with the door open. I think we both looked at each other in bewilderment. We ask her why. She tells us that Oscar has been outside our door, desperately trying to come in."

"But where was the scratching coming from?" I asked.

"Apparently Oscar got tired of sitting at the door and had gone to the next room over. He just kept scratching at the wall to let us know he was there and that he wanted to come in."

"The aide told us that he had been pacing outside our door for several hours," Rita added. "So she asked us again if we would mind leaving the door open. We looked at each other and said okay. Well, as soon as the door opens, Oscar comes charging into the room from next door at breakneck speed, and then he leaps onto the bed with our mother. He stamps out a place next to her and then looks at us with this satisfied expression on his face. Then he sits down next to her, curls up in a ball, and goes to sleep."

"We both just kept looking at each other," Annette recalled, "totally bewildered by what we were seeing."

"So, was he there when she died?"

Rita held up her hand to interrupt me. I can tell she's told this story before.

"It gets better, Dr. Dosa," she said. "The same aide came back a little later to change the bed linens. She walks up to the bed to shoo Oscar away so she can change the sheets. Oscar just looks at her, stubbornly refusing to budge. When she tried to pick him up, he hissed and swatted at her with his paw."

I thought back on my first encounter with Oscar and unconsciously rubbed my hand where he had scratched me.

"So, who won?" I asked with a smile, knowing full well how it turned out.

"Oh, Oscar did," Rita said. "The aide finally gave up. Oscar didn't leave my mother's side until she passed. In fact, he didn't leave until the undertaker arrived."

"The strangest thing," Annette recalled, "was after the undertaker came, and they were wheeling her out, Oscar stood up, like he was at attention."

"Sort of like a sentry," her sister said.

"Yeah," Annette agreed, "like a sentry."

IT'S FUNNY, but until that day I had imagined that Rita and Annette would run from the nursing home the way you might flee the scene of an accident. If anything, they seemed reluctant to go. As Rita had said, "Steere House was like our second home." While some of the affection was no doubt due to the friends they had made there over time (it was like old home week that afternoon), I also knew that some of that love came courtesy of Oscar and his four-footed friends.

"Like a bridge between the mother and daughter," Mary had said, after my visit with Donna, and I was starting to think of Oscar in that way, as a sort of gentle guide who could take people from someplace scary to one more forgiving.

I think it's one of the reasons we've kept cats at Steere House all these years. The patients like them, for the most part, either because they hark back to some forgotten relationship they may have had with a pet, or maybe because they are nonjudgmental. A cat doesn't care what you do for a living or whether you're rich or poor. A cat doesn't care if you're able to remember its name or if you're up to date with the latest news. But we were beginning to realize that cats mean something to the families, too, long before Oscar started his vigils. They seem to help reassure family members who enter into the nursing home with some trepidation. For a lot of visitors, the reality of nursing home existence can be a rather harsh wake-up call. All the more reason to take comfort in something familiar. Even if it is a cat.

CHAPTER ELEVEN

"There are two means of refuge from the miseries of life: music and cats."

ALBERT SCHWEITZER

THE FERRETTI HOUSE LOOKED LIKE ONE OF THOSE spreads you'd see in *Architectural Digest.* Situated on one of North Providence's many hills, the townhouse faced south, with a commanding view of the city through large picture windows. The layout was open and airy as one room flowed seamlessly into another. The home was decorated with modern furniture, with every surface spotless, every corner clean and well lit. Bookshelves and artwork adorned every wall.

"This was where my husband and I were going to retire," Jeanne Ferretti said to me as she gave me the tour that winter afternoon. "He loved it here."

She escorted me to the kitchen table and we sat down.

"I want you to look at this," she told me, placing a three-ringed binder in front of me on the table. "My husband was a very open person. We didn't have many secrets, but he did have a drawer where he kept his work journals. That was his private place and I respected it. It was six months after his death before I got up the nerve to look through them."

I opened the front cover of the binder and looked at the first page.

dear—
—GOD
thank—
you—

I didn't know what to make of it.

"It seems kind of strange to be coming from someone who was losing everything," Jeanne said. She was standing by the window as I sat at the table. "Turn the page."

There, similarly arranged, were three words:

JEANNE
Missy
SweetIE

"Those are nicknames he gave me over the years," she said. Terms of endearment.

I flipped to the next page and found the days of the week, Monday through Sunday, printed in block letters, one on top of the other. It was like looking at a child's primer, but one that captured some element of Lino's life and his fight against his disease. On one page the alphabet was written out twice, printed first and then written in script. There was another page of dates that had been important to him, including his anniversary, his son's birthday, Independence Day, Thanksgiving, and Christmas.

I stopped to study the next page. It was a crib sheet, the kind a grade-school child might produce in preparation for a test. Printed on the page were the answers to questions commonly found on memory examinations: the date, the season, the day of the week, the names of the president of the United States and the governor of Rhode Island.

I felt odd looking at Lino's cheat sheet, as if I were prying. I looked up at Jeanne, who was staring out the window.

"He was trying to fight it," she said after a moment, "doing battle against his undoing. I never realized how hard he fought it until after he was gone. He just didn't let me in."

She looked down at the binder and pointed to the crib notes for his doctor's exam.

"I helped him with this one. He knew he was going to the doctor and was adamant that we study these questions. We went over it for hours before the appointment. I thought he threw it out."

Jeanne shook her head and smiled wryly.

"It didn't help, though. He still missed most of the questions. I think I almost started to cry when we were there in the doctor's office and he was missing all of the questions that he so diligently studied for."

As a frequent administrator of those tests, I was surprised. It had never occurred to me that people would prep for them, try to game the system.

Jeanne took the binder from me and flipped through its pages until she found what she was looking for.

"Look at this," she said, setting it back in front of me.

The page was taken from a musical dictionary. It contained detailed definitions of various musical instruments: trumpet, piano, saxophone, trombone, and others. On the following page was a schematic picture of all the major and minor chords. At the bottom, in Lino's shaky handwriting, was the date: January 2003—more than three years before he died and at least four years after the onset of his Alzheimer's.

"My husband's world was music," she said.

TO APPRECIATE the full magnitude of a man, you need to know his whole story. Ercolino Ferretti—Lino to his friends—was born in the early part of the twentieth century to one of the thousands of first-generation Italian-American families new to the industrial suburbs of North Boston. His father scratched out a living on the railroad while his mother worked as a seamstress in one of Boston's many factories. It was a hard life, the kind shared by many of the immigrant families that built this country.

Over the course of his eighty-seven years, Lino escaped work in the factories by becoming the very definition of a renaissance man. He was a musician, and he learned to play a number of instruments with ease. Though the army temporarily took him away from his passion, Lino returned to his love of music when he returned home after World War II. He attended the prestigious New England Conservatory of Music, where several of his teachers proclaimed him one of his generation's most talented composers.

Pushing the boundaries of modern music, Lino explored complex compositions. But his pieces required 200-plus–piece ensembles, and that presented logistical problems. He needed a new framework for his music, an outlet for his unorthodox compositions. He found that platform in the developing world of computers.

Though he may not be a household name, Lino Ferretti was a pioneer. Had he pursued more conventional compositions or become an orchestral conductor as his teachers had suggested, he might be more famous today. Instead, he launched himself into computers when they were still large enough to fill a room. He taught at MIT and lectured around the world, discussing his findings with like-minded innovators. Lino was right about computers as a forum for music. Anyone who powers on a PC today or listens to an iPod knows just how much music has gone digital. But few of us know how much his research helped to make that all possible.

Lino had a curious and nimble mind that allowed him to keep up with the rapidly changing world of computers. He remained active in that field even after he retired from university life.

Then one day he was stumped.

"How do I log on?" he asked his baffled wife one morning in 2001. Suddenly, the man who had performed works of startling complexity was thrown by a simple task. Yes, he had forgotten things, missed appointments, and there was that time he couldn't make out a check, but those lapses were always so easy to dismiss.

"He's just tired," his wife had said in the past, making excuses. "He's got a lot on his mind." But the morning that her husband couldn't turn on his computer was the beginning of the end for Jeanne. It frightened her, and she immediately sought medical attention for him.

When I initially met Lino in my office a few years after he was diagnosed, he was still able to carry on a conversation and function independently at home. Two years later he was in need of twenty-four-hour care. His final year was spent at Steere House, with Jeanne his constant companion.

"I wrote in his eulogy that music was his love, life, and passion." She had moved now from the window to my side. She pointed to the page containing the musical definitions of common instruments. "This is what the disease did to him. To see the erosion of his intellect and creativity, to see it come to this . . . It was the hardest thing to endure.

"I want to play you something," Jeanne said. She walked across the adjoining living room to the stereo. The sound of a jazz quartet filled the air.

"My husband loved jazz," she said over the wail of a saxophone. "This was one of his favorite records. Even as Lino's disease progressed, he never lost his love of music."

As we listened in silence to the sound of four musicians swinging together, I thought about all of the patients I've cared for with dementia. Then I thought of my newborn daughter at home, barely six months old. There's something about music that is innate, something seemingly immune to the ravages of age-related diseases. As many new parents learn, music is sometimes the only way to comfort a screaming child. I thought back on the many late nights my daughter and I had shared recently with Johann Sebastian Bach, how the music soothed her as I rocked her to sleep. The effects can be similar for patients with dementia. Music, it seems, represents a way in—a means to communicate.

"When we lived here together, before he went to the nursing home, we would start each day with a Bach cantata or a Mozart piano concerto," Jeanne recalled. "He loved it, all of it. By the time he went to the nursing home, he no longer knew how to turn the CD player on, but I would put it on for him and he would sit in his rocking chair and listen with his eyes closed, lost in the music.

"One of the things I found most interesting about my husband's disease was that even toward the end of his life he responded to music. Here was this man who could no longer do much of anything. Sometimes he would get agitated. If you put on a jazz record, though, he would just sit contentedly in his chair for hours."

She looked at me. "Why is that? Why is Alzheimer's such a strange disease?"

"My suspicion is that certain ingrained memories never really go away," I said. "I'm convinced that there are some visceral responses that are still accessible, things that are never completely lost. For example, I know that at the end, Lino no longer knew your name. Nevertheless, I am quite sure that he knew you were important to him."

Jeanne nodded. I suspected that this was reassuring to her, or maybe it just confirmed what she already believed.

"Maybe you're right. Still, I wonder why that is?"

"I think that many of the memories are still there. They just aren't readily available. It's kind of like a computer hard drive that crashes but still maintains the files; you just can't get to them. But some things get through. I think this is why so many of the residents respond to babies, and animals like Oscar."

The mention of Oscar made Jeanne smile. "You know, my husband always loved animals, particularly cats. We had two Siamese cats before our son was born. They were our babies. Unfortunately, our son ended up being terribly allergic, so we didn't have any more after they died."

"Did Lino respond to Oscar?"

"Sure, sometimes he'd even follow the cat around the unit."

I pictured the Lino I knew—infinitely curious, filled with wonder—stalking the elusive Oscar. This was not a cat known for cuddling up with residents, remember, and I have to think that our favorite feline must have felt annoyed to find himself the object of Lino's scientific curiosity. For Lino, losing his memory, his faculties, but never his love of music, Oscar might have seemed just out of reach, that last lost chord. Or maybe he just liked chasing animals.

"Was he there at the end?"

"Yes, I think Oscar knew before the nurses did. My husband developed pneumonia. As you know, he started sliding pretty quickly and we didn't want to treat him aggressively. The day he died, I came in the afternoon. He was doing poorly, but hanging in there. One of the nurses came in and told me that she thought that Lino still had time and that I should go home. I agreed to go home to shower and eat dinner, but they called me back almost immediately. When I came back I realized that things were different. I went into the room and saw that they had dimmed the lights. Then I saw that Oscar was there, sitting on the bed holding his own private vigil.

"I guess I knew then. I'd heard about the cat from others on the floor. I called my son and told him to come in. It wasn't until he arrived that I remembered his allergies. I asked him if he wanted me to send Oscar away."

She smiled ever so slightly.

"My son was definitive. 'No,' he said, 'Dad loved cats and would have been happy with Oscar on the bed with him.' He told me he would be okay."

We sat in silence for a while, listening to the music again. Jeanne looked out the window at a bird that had landed on her feeder just outside, but the feeder was empty, and the bird didn't stay long. As it flew off Jeanne looked back at me. Her expression had changed; the wistful memory of her son was replaced by a look of grave seriousness.

"To see someone you love go away like my husband did . . . that's the hardest thing."

Jeanne wiped her brow with the tissue she had been holding.

"I'm so grateful for the time we had, the good times before . . . I wouldn't trade those years for anything, but I still haven't gotten to the point where I can see him the way he used to be before the illness."

There was nothing I could add. I was there to learn and listen.

After a moment she said, "I suppose that's what marriage vows are all about—in good times and bad?"

She looked over at the digital frame that sat on her kitchen table. Pictures of her grandchildren came in and out of view, a twenty-first-century slide show.

"My son gave me that for Christmas," she said. I looked over and saw a picture of her grandson, seemingly suspended in midair on a sled, his face a study in exhilaration. It was the kind of photo parents and grandparents everywhere treasure, the purity of childhood with none of the complexities that come later in life.

She pointed at the image and looked back at me.

"Enjoy these times," she said, her final instruction of the day. "They're gone in a blink of an eye." Then she got up from her chair to grab some more cookies from the kitchen counter.

"Now, enough about me and my husband. Tell me about your kids."

WHEN I WALKED THROUGH the front door of my house that night, I was greeted by the high-pitched squeal of my son, Ethan, who raced out of the kitchen, arms open wide to greet me. His face contained the most unalloyed expression of joy imaginable: All I had to do to make his day was come home. I picked him up and squeezed him tight.

"How's my big boy?" I said, and after kissing my cheek he launched into a breathless and slightly incomprehensible explanation of everything he had done that day.

"Daddy, you'll never guess what I saw today at school."

"What?"

"I can't tell you . . . it's a secret."

It was a familiar game we played and it was my job to guess.

"Was it a spaceship?"

He looked at me with his large brown eyes opened wide.

"Noooooo, Daddy."

"Was it . . . A DINOSAUR?"

"Noooooo, Daddy."

"Was it a—?"

Unable to contain himself any longer, Ethan blurted out, "It was a fire truck! And it was big and red and it made a lot of noise."

The exchange continued as I carried him into the living room where I was greeted by the sight of my beautiful wife lying on the carpet beside our newborn daughter. When Dionne saw me she flashed the same smile I fell in love with all those years ago, and for an instant I thought our daughter Emma even emulated her. These were the riches I had, and I wasn't going to wait until I retired to count them either. In good times and bad.

CHAPTER TWELVE

"Time spent with cats is never wasted."

COLETTE

I WAS LOOKING FORWARD TO DEBRIEFING MARY ON MY conversation with Mrs. Ferretti, but that would have to wait. It was already 4:30 and the day shift had left. My office staff had called me earlier in the day to inform me that I had a new patient to see. As I made my way toward the elevators, a familiar voice flagged me down.

"Hey, you," Ida said from her wheelchair. "Where are you off to in such a hurry?"

"I've got long legs, Ida," I joked, "and lots of places to go."

"Yeah, I remember those days. Too many appointments, not enough time to get it all done. It all seemed so important at the time."

"Is this your way of telling me to slow down?"

"You've got to enjoy the journey, Dr. Dosa. Savor the moment."

It was like Ida had been reading my mail. "It's funny," I said, "but the wife of a former patient of mine was just telling me the same thing."

"Former as in 'dead'?"

Ida was never one to beat around the bush. I nodded. "One of my patients on the third floor. This woman realized after her husband was gone how precious the good times were. Those times when everything seemed just normal."

Ida grimaced a bit as if to say, *Tell me about it*. But instead she turned her focus on me.

"What about those kids of yours?" she asked. "You spending enough time with them?"

"I'm trying my best."

"You got any pictures for me? Why don't you sit down for a second?"

I pulled up a chair and then proudly pulled out my PDA.

"What is that thing, one of those new-fangled contraptions I see everyone carrying around? I suppose you've got your whole life on there."

"Pretty much," I said. I pulled up a few recent shots: my son's birthday party, my daughter's first smile.

"You realize, don't you, that raising those kids is the most important thing you'll ever do? Much more important than any of those grants you apply for or even any of your patients—except me, of course."

"I always have time for you, Ida."

"Then tell me what you're learning about our friend Oscar."

I looked at her quizzically. Maybe she *had* been reading my mail. Ida laughed. "Mary told me. She likes to keep me in the loop. So, what have you found out?"

I thought for a minute before offering an answer. "I feel like the more I learn, the less I know. I mean, why does he do it?"

"Who knows, Dr. Dosa? There's probably some scientific explanation but in the end, does it really matter? He's there when it counts."

"I guess," I said. "But I come from a family of scientists. We don't care so much if there is a genie in the bottle as how he got in there."

"You're supposed to be thinking what wish you want granted," she said with a laugh. "Are you a man of faith, Doctor?"

"Well, I don't believe in genies, if that's what you mean." Actually faith and religion are topics I've never been very comfortable talking about. "If you're asking me if I went to a church or synagogue growing up, the answer is no. My father was a Catholic choirboy when he was a kid, and my mother was Jewish, but they raised us to be pretty agnostic."

"How about your wife?"

"Well, she's from a Protestant family. I always joke that if we raise a Buddhist and a Muslim we'll have the major religions covered."

"You're forgetting the Hindus," said Ida with a laugh. "They're the ones who believe in reincarnation."

"You're right. I guess I'll have to have a third child," I said chuckling. I glanced over and pointed to Munchie, sprawled out fast asleep on the piano bench. "If we're lucky, Ida, maybe we'll both come back as cats in another life."

"Yeah, they certainly lead the good life in here."

"In all seriousness, Ida, if you're asking me whether I believe there is a deeper meaning to our time here on earth, I'd have to say yes. At least I hope there is. You can't do this job without accepting that there are many mysteries in medicine that go well beyond the science we learn in medical school."

With that, I stood up. "Unfortunately, I've got to go upstairs now."

"You're seeing that new woman up on three," she said with some certainty.

"I should just hire you as my secretary."

"You could. I make it my business to know what's going on around here, Dr. Dosa." She gestured with her head toward the elevator. "I saw the medics bring her in here about three hours ago. She didn't look so good. You better get up there before Oscar does."

IDA GOT ME THINKING, as she often did. This time it was of my own first encounter with the unexplained. As a young resident at the University of Pittsburgh, I had gone into a hospital room one morning to see a patient who had been admitted with what appeared to be a mild case of pneumonia.

Even at her worst, my patient was a beautiful woman. Young and vital, with long blonde hair and striking blue eyes, this thirty-something woman could have graced the cover of a fashion magazine. But on that morning she looked pale and frightened.

"So, how are you doing?" I asked, with forced bonhomie. I was new at this doctor thing and trying to make up for my lack of experience with what I thought to be a winning bedside manner. In reality, I probably just looked like a cad.

She had looked at me as if she were trying to decide whether or not to trust me. She was fidgeting, shifting her weight on the bed while nervously twirling her long hair between her thumb and forefinger.

"To be honest," she said after a moment, "I feel okay. But I woke up this morning dreaming that I was going to die today. I keep trying to tell myself it was just a dream but frankly, I'm scared out of my mind." I thought she might cry. "I know it's silly," she said.

I tried to remember what, if anything, they had taught us about completely irrational fear. I put my hand on her shoulder. I was doing my best to impersonate a doctor.

"You really don't need to worry," I told her. "You're so much better. In fact, I think we're going to be sending you home today. The antibiotics should take care of the rest and you'll be back to normal in a few days."

She acknowledged the news with a nod, but there was no expression of relief.

"That must have been some dream," I said. "Let me take a look at you." I might have been new to doctoring, but I knew that listening to my patient's fear was the most likely way to break the tension. I mean, don't we all want to be heard, to feel that our fears—no matter how apparently outlandish—are taken seriously?

Doing something seemed to help. As I examined her I felt her relax. I took her blood pressure and listened to her heart and lungs. At each step of my head-to-toe exam, I told her that I could find nothing wrong save for the now faint signs of pneumonia lingering in her left lower lung. By the time I was done she was smiling again.

"Thank you, Doctor," she said at the end. "I guess I just need to get out of here."

I left the room feeling quite pleased with myself. What a good doctor I was turning out to be.

Three hours later, I received a 911 call.

"Who is it?" I asked the nurse, my heart leaping into my throat.

"I don't know," she replied. "I'm just relaying the message from the patient's nurse. But you better hurry."

As I raced to the same floor where I had visited my young patient, I tried to convince myself that it couldn't be her. There were so many sicker, older patients on the same floor. The eighty-five-year-old woman with lung cancer. The brittle diabetic with the recent heart attack.

I ran toward the nurse's desk where an aide directed me down the hallway, away from my young patient's room. I had a perverse sense of relief: It was somebody else. I left the aide behind and rounded the corner at high speed. Like a football player shedding tackles in his opponent's backfield, I raced past the parked EKG machine and a dietary cart filled with the remnants of that morning's breakfast. As I passed the last obstacle I could see someone lying on the ground at the far end of the hallway. Slowing my pace to allow my heart to stop racing, I approached the patient.

It was her.

She was crumpled on the floor in a fetal position, facing the wall. Though I couldn't see her face, her long blonde hair was unmistakable. I stood there, paralyzed.

"Doctor, do you want me to call the rescue team?" a voice asked.

It was Judy, an experienced nurse of many years, racing down the hallway toward me, wheeling an oxygen container behind her. I didn't answer. I was still in shock.

"Doctor!"

I snapped back. "What happened?" I asked.

Nervously, Judy began filling me in. "We told her to take a walk this morning, to get some exercise before going home. All of a sudden she collapsed. By the time I got here she was struggling to breathe."

Judy then reeled off the vital signs, which I acknowledged before kneeling down beside my patient. As I rolled her over away from the wall, I could see that her face was ashen, her eyes filled with tears. Her chest heaved as if she were fighting against some unknown compressive force. As I leaned down to her level, our eyes met. I saw an expression—fear, betrayal, accusation—that is with me to this day. That look will be with me always.

"I can't breathe," she told me, gasping for air.

I looked up at Judy and told her to call the rescue team. Then I looked over my patient and tried to calm her.

"You're going to be fine," I said. "The cavalry's coming."

This time I was the one who was scared; she could hear it in my voice. She began to sob. I placed my hands under her arms and propped her up against the wall of the hallway. Then I applied oxygen from the portable tank and slumped down beside her. For a moment, she appeared to improve.

Color returned to her face and the vigorous heaving of her chest seemed to calm. I allowed myself to relax for a moment. We would get through this.

"You'll be okay," I told her, attempting to smile.

I could hear a stampede of physicians racing down the hall toward my patient. "I told you they would come." She looked at me again. This time however her gaze was vacant. Then her eyes rolled up into her head and she slumped back onto the floor. Amid the sounds of shouting health care workers, I began cardiac resuscitation. After a few minutes of chest compressions I backed off, exhausted, breathlessly allowing one of my colleagues to take over. I stood watching the cardiac arrest unfold, with doctors shouting and nurses scrambling for supplies.

She had been scared. Why hadn't I ordered more tests? Why hadn't I stayed with her? Thirty minutes later, we abandoned our efforts and I was pronouncing a woman dead who had told me earlier in the day that she was going to die. Every part of my exam had been normal, but she had known different.

How had she known?

An autopsy a few days later would tell us that a large blood clot had traveled to her lungs. It also told us she had a rare, previously undiagnosed blood disorder that predisposed her to her terrible fate. In the end, there was a scientific explanation as to why she had died that morning—but how to explain her dream?

I've seen a lot of strange things since then. There was the man who presented with disseminated cancer only to have the disease disappear a year later, despite refusing aggressive treatment. He was someone who was *supposed* to die—but didn't. Then there was the man who insisted on being admitted because "something was wrong" despite every test to the contrary. We tried to discharge him, but he refused to leave. We all thought he was crazy and even ordered psychiatric testing until the third day of his hospital stay when his cardiac monitor finally captured the life-threatening arrhythmia that was causing his symptoms. Like my young patient he had *known*—and probably wouldn't be with us anymore had he listened to the experts.

Then there was the elderly woman who announced to me on December 31, 1999, that she had accomplished her objective of living to the turn of the century. "I'm going to die today, Doctor," she told me quite casually. Every test showed she had nothing wrong. No infections, heart problems—nothing that might lead directly to her death. She simply came to the hospital because she was ready to die. As she foretold, she did die several hours later of unknown causes.

Science has taken us a long way in our profession, but we still just scratch the surface. The rest remains a mystery. Maybe some people just know when their time has come. Some cats, too.

CHAPTER THIRTEEN

"The cat has too much spirit to have no heart."

ERNEST MENAUL

I HAD THE CHART FOR OUR NEW CHARGE. MRS. ARELLA Matos was a ninety-year-old woman with Alzheimer's disease and a laundry list of medical diagnoses and medications. This was my introduction to someone I probably wouldn't know for long.

I went to Mrs. Matos's room and found her three daughters there, gathered close together as if in prayer. Behind them their mother lay sleeping. Her breathing was fast and she looked uncomfortable. A young boy sat on the bed next to her, playing with a pair of action figures. He had one in each hand and they were fighting each other.

"Hello," I said to the family. "I'm Dr. Dosa."

I introduced myself to each of the daughters, Gabriella, Caterina, and Ana. As I shook their hands, I studied each of their faces. You can learn a lot from faces, particularly the eyes. Happiness, worry, excitement, fear—it all shows up there. The eyes of these three women were filled with a profound sadness. Whether they had admitted it to themselves or not, these dutiful daughters knew their mother had arrived at her last stop.

"Who's this?" I asked, referring to the little boy. He was no more than five and he reminded me of my own son. Gabriella, the daughter I presumed to be the oldest, answered.

"That's my son, Freddy."

I walked over and sat down on the bed next to him.

"Hi there, Freddy. I'm Doctor Dosa. How old are you?"

Freddy put up one hand to indicate that he was indeed five years old. Then he showed me his action figures.

"This is Spider-Man and this is Superman."

"Are they helping to take care of your grandmother?"

Freddy nodded and then slipped back into his pretend world, pitting the two action figures against each other in mock combat.

I turned my attention to the daughters.

"Tell me about your mother."

Gabriella was the first to speak. "Doctor, we feel terrible about moving our mother from home. She always told us . . ." Her voice trailed off and became almost inaudible. I moved in closer.

"It just got to be too much for us to take care of her," Caterina said, picking up where her sister left off.

They probably felt like they had let their mother down by not heeding her wishes. Looking at Mrs. Matos and her degree of discomfort, I was reminded that circumstances sometimes make that wish impossible.

An aide entered the room to do her admissions assessment. I suggested that we relocate to the family room down the hall so we could talk. The youngest daughter, Ana, launched into an explanation.

"Our mother was always fiercely independent. She stayed to herself so we didn't see it coming until it was too late. Three years ago, Caterina and I went back to our country, the Dominican Republic, to see her. Her apartment was a complete disaster. Newspapers were everywhere, unwashed dishes sat in the sink. It was clear she hadn't washed her clothes."

Ana looked over at Caterina and I could sense that they were reliving the memory together.

"Doctor, we both went outside and just started to cry. My mother had always taken such pride in her home. You couldn't put so much as a coffee cup on the table without her taking it away to rinse it. And now? How could we let our mother live this way? Right there we decided to move her to the United States and we put her on a plane with us. That was two years ago. Since then, we've done the best we could to take care of her, but—"

Ana put her hands up toward her head as the history became too much for her to relate.

Gabriella picked up the story. "When my mother got to Rhode Island, she became confused. Her English was not very good, and I think the language barrier only added to her confusion. She had no idea where she was. At night, she would get up and wander. One time we even had to call the police to help us find her. You can't imagine how frightening it is to wake up and realize that your mother isn't there. One night about a year ago, she walked out of my sister's house and fell down the stairs. She didn't get hurt—thank God!—so they sent her home from the ER. No one ever suggested we needed help or offered us any advice."

Caterina jumped in. "A few weeks later, my mother stopped eating. Then she developed pneumonia. Each time, we talked to her primary care doctor and he just sent us home. She's depressed, he told me, and he gave us a medication. She has pneumonia, he told Gabriella, so here's an antibiotic. He just gave us pills. None of us knew what to do. We started sleeping next to our mother on the floor to make sure she wouldn't get up in the middle of the night. It was just so exhausting. Finally, a few months ago, Mom stopped walking so I had to ask my doctor to send a physical therapist to help us. When the therapist arrived, she took one look around and asked why we didn't have hospice involved. I was stunned. I remember calling up my sister that night and asking her why the therapist would ask us about hospice. It seems silly now, but honestly, none of us even considered that Mom was dying. The next day, I contacted our doctor and asked him about it. He told me he hadn't even thought about hospice."

The months of frustration had taken their toll. "I wish doctors would let people know that hospices are there for other things besides dying from cancer," Gabriella said. "People hear the word *hospice* and go, 'Oh, they're terminal. They're dying of cancer.' But my mother isn't dying of cancer. She has dementia."

I felt sorry for the Matos family. It seemed particularly tragic that the family would have to learn about hospice through a random comment like that. But many doctors don't consider hospice until the very end because they don't understand the concept themselves. They don't realize that hospice care isn't limited to hanging a morphine drip at the end of life. It can be an indispensable resource, a well of support throughout.

Hospice workers provide more than information on the physical act of dying; they offer practical and emotional guidance. Hospice can often provide the necessary custodial care and nursing support needed to keep patients at home as their diseases get worse, services that can actually sometimes extend a life.

"I'm sorry that you had to go through all of this," I said. "Hopefully we'll be able to help your mother pass peacefully."

"We wanted to keep our mother at home, Doctor, honestly." Gabriela spoke for the three of them.

I nodded. I understood their situation better than they might have imagined. Hearing their description of their mother's unkempt home, I thought of my own mother-in-law and the last visit my wife and I had paid her. My wife and I appeared to be headed down an identical path to that of the family in front of me and their experiences left me with a sense of dread for what the days ahead might hold for the two of us.

"The good news is that your mother's here right now and you're with her," I said to the Matos sisters. "That's what counts."

BACK IN MRS. MATOS'S ROOM a hospice nurse had arrived to evaluate her. She was not the only visitor, though. The darkness of the window reflected the unmistakable silhouette of a cat perched above the bed. Oscar had arrived. He ignored us, focusing on his patient instead. Then he settled in, turning himself around—once, twice, three times—before sitting down with his head on his paws. By the looks of it, he appeared to be staying.

Freddy noticed.

"Look, Mama, there's a cat."

I looked at the boy. For the first time his face was animated, excitement in his eyes.

"That's Oscar," I said.

"Does he live here?" the child asked, walking over to get a closer look.

"Yes, Oscar lives with all the other people on the floor."

"What does he do?"

"Well, mostly cat things, but I guess he also takes care of everyone."

"Will he take care of my grandma while she's here?"

"Yes, Freddy, he will. Would you like that?"

Freddy thought for a moment before responding with a solemn yes.

I wondered if a five-year-old could truly comprehend what was going on. Could he grasp the finality of his grandmother's situation? Probably not. My own son was just now starting to grapple with the idea of death. I recalled a recent conversation with Ethan while I was tucking him into bed. "Dad," he asked, "when I die, will I go to college?"

Still, Freddy seemed relieved by the thought of a cat helping his grandmother. He offered his hand to the cat. Oscar sniffed at it and for a second I cringed, but Oscar didn't seem bothered. He allowed the boy to pet him, and even seemed to enjoy it.

I guess I'll never really understand cats.

The hospice nurse finished her assessment of Mrs. Matos and introduced herself to the daughters. I used this as my opportunity to leave, offering my good-byes. I knew I wouldn't see them again.

As I left the room to take care of my own paperwork I heard a voice behind me.

"Doctor!"

I turned to see Caterina. "Thank you for your time, Doctor, but I have one last question. We have a fourth sister, Maria, who lives in California. She's used up so much of her sick time to help us care for our mother. Do you think we should tell her to fly in?"

I looked past her into the room. Through the door I could see the silhouette of Oscar, sitting quietly on the bed. He was still receiving affection from his new friend.

"Yes," I said to Caterina with certainty, "you should all be here."

CHAPTER FOURTEEN

"Dogs have owners. Cats have staff."

UNKNOWN

AS AN EARLY WARNING SYSTEM, OSCAR'S AVERAGE WAS proving to be uncanny. "What do you think would happen if we had two patients who were dying at the same time?" I asked Mary one afternoon not long after Mrs. Matos had passed away.

"That actually happened!" she said. We were sitting in her office behind the front desk and the third floor was very quiet. "They were both going; it was hard to say who was going to die first. But one of them was very comfortable; you remember your patient, Larry Scheer?"

I nodded as Mary continued.

"At any rate, Larry was a hospice patient and he was doing okay. But this other gentleman, he was all the way over on the other side of the ward and having a real tough time of it. He had great trouble breathing and couldn't get comfortable. That's who Oscar chose to be with!"

"As if he could tell he was having the more difficult time."

Mary nodded. "His poor wife was there, watching all of this unfold. I remember walking down the hallway to see her, thinking how terrible it must be for her, but she was accepting of the situation. I asked her if there was anything I could do and she told me that Oscar was there for her husband and that they both would be okay."

"It sounds like Oscar was distracting her from a pretty miserable scene."

Mary smiled at the memory. "I guess," she said. "At one point, I think she even broke out her camera to take a picture of Oscar." The idea of a positive memory in the midst of such a bleak scene was strangely comforting.

I looked down the hall, searching for the cat in question. Maya was curled up on a chair behind the desk, but no Oscar.

"Speaking of," I said, "where is he?"

"He was with one of your colleagues' patients last night and I guess he's just wiped out. He disappeared somewhere. It's like he hibernates."

"Does he eat when he's on the job?"

"Sometimes . . . but it's not like he dawdles. He'll slip out for two minutes, grab some kibble, and then he's back at the patient's side. It's like he's literally on a vigil."

I was imagining Oscar sleeping somewhere, perhaps in a closet or under a bed. "What do you think it's about, Mary?" I asked. "Why does he do what he does?"

"I thought that's what you were trying to find out by talking to the families."

"Partly. But as they say, peel an onion . . . I'm curious: What's your take?"

She sat back in her chair and mused for a moment. "Well, you know, Oscar is my baby. He bonded to me right away. I would give him his ice water every morning."

"Man, these cats are spoiled! Nobody brings me ice water."

Mary smiled but then turned serious. "If you've ever had a pet, you know that when someone in your family is in trouble, the pet will usually go and stay with them."

I thought back on Jolly, the black miniature poodle that kept me company when I was sick as a child. "True," I said. "But that's different. My dog was part of our family."

"Well, what do you think this is?" Mary said. "This is Oscar's home. He has forty-one family members and when one of them is in trouble, he goes and stays with them."

I was quiet for a minute, thinking of the one cat that seemed to care for the forty-one residents on this floor. No wonder he was exhausted.

"So, who else are you going to talk to?" Mary asked, changing the subject.

"I don't know. I guess there are still a number of people on my list to interview. Based on your story, I suppose Mrs. Scheer should be on the list. And I still have to get in touch with Jack McCullough . . ."

The call bell rang at the front desk, interrupting us mid-conversation. Mary leaned over and hit the button.

"Can I help you?"

Frank Rubenstein's unmistakable voice answered.

"Mary, I need you. Can you look at my wife?"

Our conversation had come to an end.

"I guess it's time to go back to work," she announced as she disappeared down the hall.

I grabbed Ruth Rubenstein's chart off the rack. Ruth had recently been readmitted after a weeklong hospital stay for a bout with pneumonia.

Her infection had quickly improved in the hospital, but the change in environments left her confused and delirious. She stopped eating and needed powerful medications to help keep her calm. Eventually, a one-to-one aide was required just to keep Ruth from getting out of bed and falling in the middle of the night.

As I reviewed Ruth's hospital records, I became aware of a presence. I was not alone. Oscar had materialized as if from nowhere, and was sitting on the ground next to me giving me the fish eye.

"What?" I said. "Am I in your spot again?"

He meowed—softly at first, but more forcefully each time.

"You're in his way," Mary announced with a chuckle as she returned from Frank's room. She pointed down to the water bowl beneath the desk. "Your feet are in his way."

"My apologies, Your Highness," I said standing up. Eyeing me suspiciously, Oscar waited until I had moved to the other side of the desk before tiptoeing in to have a drink.

"Would you look at that?" I cried.

"It's his desk, David; just be happy that he lets you work here from time to time." It was becoming her new mantra. This was Oscar's world.

"Frank wants to see you," Mary said, bringing me back to reality. I looked at her for more explanation.

"Ruth's been too confused to eat anything since she came back. We've tried to sit with her—you know, to get her to take something—but she won't take a bite. He's been out here at least a half dozen times this morning already asking how he can get her to eat. The last time I told him that she would eat when she's *ready* to eat. I even tried to reassure him by saying that she was still receiving IV fluids and that was helping."

"How did he react to that?"

"He nearly bit my head off! Then he walked off muttering that I wanted his wife to die."

It's never easy for family members to watch their loved ones refuse to eat. Eating is essential to life, and families at the nursing home often use it as a barometer for how someone is doing, never mind the fact that everybody's appetite varies from time to time.

"So, what did he want just now?" I asked.

"Same thing. He wanted to know if I could get her to eat her lunch. She didn't touch a thing."

On my way toward Ruth's room I passed Louise, asleep in a hallway chair, her walker parked carefully by her side. As usual, she was meticulously groomed: Her white hair had been cut and delicately curled. Her off-white blouse was paired with a skirt that modestly covered her knees. She looked peaceful, as if she had fallen asleep during a church service with thoughts of salvation in her head. Not for the first time I wondered, What was she dreaming of?

It's a big question. Do people with dementia dream as they once did, or are their dreams disordered and fretful, a by-product of their disease? Do their dreams offer a respite from the confusion of their waking state, or do they contribute to it? It's something I've wondered a lot about. After all, many scientists have suggested that dreaming is critical to learning—it's the brain's chance to reorganize itself, to process memories, and perhaps store them away so they can be accessed later. So, what does that mean for the patient with memory impairment?

And what about the medications? In early dementia, patients are often treated with Alzheimer's drugs that increase acetylcholine levels in the brain, which can lead to profound and sometimes disturbing dreams. Yet in later stages of the disease, you hear less and less about patients' dreams. Perhaps they cease to be as important or memorable. Perhaps they lose the recollection of even those. Still, as I watched Louise softly snoring, I hoped she was at peace in her dream world, and that some of the memories she had lost access to in her waking life were restored to her in sleep.

Was she dreaming about her husband, the handsome flyer in his World War II uniform forever ready to launch or just returned from some sortie? I tried to imagine Louise's life then, what it must have been like to love someone who had gone off to fight—the loneliness and the fear. Maybe she was dreaming of that, or of his return from the war. Perhaps she was reliving her unbridled joy at seeing him alive and safe, a young family reunited, ready to resume the lives that history interrupted. It was heartbreaking even to consider it.

There are some memories that should never be lost. Are they found again in dreams?

RUTH WAS LYING IN BED, her eyes shut. From the look of it though, she didn't appear to be sleeping as she writhed around fitfully. Unlike Louise outside in the hallway, there were no pleasant dreams here, I was quite confident about that. I knocked on the inside of the door to announce my arrival. My knocking startled Ruth, and she opened her eyes. Frank, seemingly dozing himself, jumped to his feet and looked around.

"Oh! Dr. Dosa, I'm so glad you're here." I could hear the worry in his voice.

"How is she doing?" I asked as I walked to Ruth's bedside.

"Not good, Doctor. She's really not herself. I'm not even sure why they sent her out of the hospital. She's still very confused."

I pulled up a chair and sat down next to Frank.

"She's delirious, Mr. Rubenstein."

"What does that mean? Is her pneumonia still there?"

"No, that's been treated. But sometimes, when older people get sick, their infections can cause them to become increasingly confused. 'Delirium' is the term we use to describe that confusion. It's a change in the way patients pay attention and focus. It's why Ruth is so agitated right now."

He looked at me with a blank stare. I tried another tack.

"Her condition is similar to that of a small child who might see spiders on the wall if they have a high fever. Older people, particularly when they have memory problems like your wife, are prone to becoming confused when they have even innocent infections that wouldn't have affected them before. We call this delirium and it can persist even after the infection goes away."

"Will she get better?"

"I expect that she will get better over time, but it might take several days or even weeks."

"But she's not eating, Doctor!"

Ruth moaned from her bed. I took this as an opportunity to examine her. Sitting beside her on the bed, I placed my stethoscope on her chest. She resisted immediately, lifting up the upper half of her body while swatting at me forcefully with her hand. Frank jumped up from his chair and got on his knees next to his wife's bed. He took her hand and held it tight to his own chest. His face was filled with concern.

"The doctor's here, Ruth," he said. His tone was beseeching. "He's here to make you feel better."

I felt bad for Frank. There was actually little I could do to make her feel better other than treating her baseline infection. Despite all of the modern miracles in medicine, time alone would fix Ruth—as much as she could be fixed.

Still, her husband's reassuring voice seemed to calm her and she settled back down onto the bed. I continued my exam.

"What about the eating, Doctor? How do I get her to eat?"

"You may not be able to get her to eat right now, Frank."

"But if she doesn't eat, she's going to die!" He glared at me in frustration. "Do you want her to die?"

"No one wants her to die, Frank."

"How can she get better without nourishment?"

I sat down in the chair and measured my response.

"Frank, we are doing the best we can with feeding her given her current confusion. The nurses and the aides are trying their best. They sit with her at every meal and patiently try to feed her. I'm sure a little of it is getting in. She's also getting hydration through her IV fluids, which are providing some sustenance. When her delirium improves, I think she'll start to eat again."

"But we fixed her infection, Doctor."

"We did, but the resulting confusion takes time to improve." I felt as if I were saying the same things over and over.

"Well, if she's not going to eat, shouldn't we put in a feeding tube?"

Frank's frustration had changed to pleading.

"Frank, I don't think it would change the overall outcome. Besides, when your wife was still able to speak her mind she told me she didn't want a feeding tube to help her with her nutrition. Shouldn't we honor her wishes?"

Suddenly, I realized how thankful I was that the three of us had discussed this matter in the early days of Ruth's dementia, while she could still participate in conversations regarding her future. Of all the things I talk about with my patients and their families, the discussion about feeding tubes is perhaps the hardest. I have seen families literally ripped apart by the often agonizing decision of whether or not to insert a feeding tube into a dementia patient who has begun to lose weight. Part of what makes these conversations so hard is the common misconception that feeding tubes prolong life. In reality, there is really no place for feeding tubes in terminal dementia. Objectively, they have never been shown to increase a person's length of life or reduce the number of episodes of pneumonia. Feeding tubes are not without their side effects: They require a surgical procedure or endoscopy to insert them in the first place; they fall out easily, requiring ER visits simply to put them back in again; and they can get infected or become blocked.

There's another factor that makes conversations about feeding tubes difficult. Many people feel that not feeding patients is tantamount to cruel and unusual punishment. Unfortunately, loss of weight at the end of life is a natural byproduct of the body shutting down as it prepares itself for death. Patients at this stage of life do not perceive hunger or thirst the way someone who is healthy experiences it. But it's never easy to convince family members of this as their loved ones are fading away. It's infinitely easier when the patient has consciously weighed in on the matter at a more opportune time.

Frank looked at me with a guilty expression.

"You're right, Doctor. She did say that she didn't want a tube. She's got to eat, though. How can she get better if she doesn't eat?"

Tears came to Frank's eyes. They streamed down his face and he wiped them away with the back of his shirtsleeve.

"Hopefully, she'll start eating soon, Frank. In the meantime, we will continue to give her intravenous fluids and try to feed her what we can. We just have to hope for the best."

"But if that doesn't work?" he asked. The desperation was back.

I looked at him and tried to think of something positive to say. My face must have said it all. Frank started to sob.

I crossed the room and grabbed a box of tissues. I handed them to Frank and sat back down again. He took one and dabbed at his face.

"Doctor, I'm not ready for her to go," he said after a brief silence.

"I know you love her greatly, Frank. Unfortunately, this is how it happens. This is how patients with dementia eventually die."

Frank looked up at me and again began to cry.

I put my hand on his shoulder but there was nothing more to say.

CHAPTER FIFTEEN

"If there is one spot of sun spilling onto the floor, a cat will find it and soak it up."

J. A. MCINTOSH

MOST MORNINGS I OPERATE ON AUTOPILOT. I GET OUT OF bed, jump in the shower, and get dressed without giving any of it much thought. I use the time to plan my day, figure out whether I can stop to eat breakfast, decide where I need to go and what I need to do. It's the way most of us begin our day, relying on routine and the body to know what it needs to do while we scheme and dream.

As I watched my two children learn to walk, bathe, and feed themselves, I thought of how difficult these activities are to master. Walking doesn't begin with that first step. It begins with an awkward roll, followed by an excited crawl, then a grasp for a chair leg, and more than a few bumps and bruises before that first momentous and life-changing step. Then of course there's no stopping them.

We spend the first few years of our lives learning how to do these core activities and then we move on, never giving them another thought. For most of our lives we accept the ability to take care of ourselves as a given—until a health care issue robs us or a loved one of these primal skills. When that health care issue is dementia, we wonder if we'll ever take anything for granted again.

As the dementia patient unlearns how to perform the basic functions of life, we quickly find out just how difficult it is to bathe a 189-pound man who offers no assistance. We learn that the very act of transferring someone onto the toilet can become a multiperson job. We also discover just how much patience is required to painstakingly feed a parent who has lost all vestiges of her appetite—or even an understanding of what to do with a spoon.

It's at the middle stages of dementia—when patients gradually begin to lose the ability to care for themselves independently—that they and their families begin to fall through the cracks of our health care system. Some seek assistance from worthy organizations such as the Alzheimer's Association. Others look to friends or family with previous experience. They may seek information and support from a variety of sources—but rarely do they get it from the doctor.

Unfortunately, our health care system is built largely on a model of diagnosis and treatment. As medical students and young doctors we learn to assimilate signs and symptoms of disease, attach a label or name to it, and then suggest treatment courses based on the particular diagnosis. What do you do, though, when there are no medications to give or no surgeries to perform?

What do you do when there is no cure?

• • •

"HOW DID I THINK IT WOULD END?"

Joan Scheer was sitting in her kitchen. I watched as she nervously stroked her hair and her brown eyes became watery. I had seen a lot of people crying since I embarked on this listening tour and I had to keep reminding myself that it was intended to be cathartic—perhaps even good for them. But it didn't make me feel any better. "I suppose I thought my husband would go on the way he was." Joan's daughter, Robin, passed her a tissue. "I knew he had dementia but I thought that things wouldn't change, that each morning I would continue to drive him to his adult day care center, where they would care for him until four o'clock. Then he'd come home and I'd feed him dinner, watch TV, and then we'd go to bed. I suppose I thought that we would keep this routine going until one day when he would die of old age. I guess I was naïve, but I just didn't expect it to end the way it did."

The way it ended with Lawrence Scheer is the way it ends with most of the patients on Steere House's third floor. Mr. Scheer died at the nursing home, dutifully accompanied by Oscar, after a prolonged battle with Alzheimer's dementia. The last years of Larry's life were not kind. He began to wander at home, particularly at night, and eventually fell down the stairs. In the hospital, he seemed to deteriorate overnight. He became nonverbal and delirious, pulling his cast off three times before being strapped to the bed for his own protection. He was transferred from one nursing home to another before landing at Steere House. There, he continued to unlearn everything until, in the end, he could no longer walk, talk, or even recognize his family. He ultimately died from pneumonia.

"You know, I wish the doctors had told me what to expect."

"What do you mean?" I asked.

"They really didn't tell me anything about the disease or what it would do to my husband." She smiled at me through the tears. "You know how I found out how long a patient with Alzheimer's lives after they are diagnosed?"

I shook my head.

"My husband told me!"

She laughed at the absurdity of it.

"About a year or two after he was diagnosed, we were at a friend's house for dinner. It turned out he also had dementia and they had a book about Alzheimer's lying around on their coffee table. He started reading it. I came into the room and saw him sitting there with the book turned over on his lap. I asked him what he was doing and he told me point blank that he had about six more years to live."

Now she was the one shaking her head.

"He held up the book to show me and I was horrified! I raced over to Larry and took it from him. He looked at me and, very matter-of-fact, told me that based on his age at diagnosis, he had about seven to nine years—and that he had already lived for two of those years."

"But your doctors hadn't said anything about life expectancy to either of you?"

Joan leaned back in her chair. "Well, the doctors were always good with labeling. They would tell me that Larry had an Alzheimer's-type variant, but none of them ever sat me down and said, 'Your husband has dementia and here is what is going to happen to him step by step, year by year.' Instead, they would hold an X-ray in the air and talk to me about tangles and plaques as if I had been in medical school along with them. The X-rays didn't mean anything to me."

Unfortunately, I hear this all the time. I appreciate that physicians are trying to share information with patients and their families, but there are better ways of helping them cope with the disease.

Joan played with a napkin as she considered her next statement. It was as if she was sending a message through me. "I just wish there were more people in the medical community who could help guide you through the day-in and day-out aspects of living with someone with dementia."

"IT'S ALL ABOUT FUNCTION," a lecturer said in a class at medical school many years ago.

She paused for emphasis and looked out at the future physicians assembled before her.

"In medicine, doctors often make the mistake of pursuing diagnoses. I'm here to tell you that the name of the disease doesn't matter. It may seem important to us as physicians and many patients may think it's important, but I can guarantee you that in most cases it's irrelevant. Do you think a patient really cares if he has progressive supranuclear palsy, Alzheimer's, Pick's disease, or Lewy body dementia?"

Someone in the front row raised his hand. "But aren't all of these things important to know?"

"To the physician, they're very important," she said. "They're the language we use to convey information to one another.

They help us define an illness and talk to each other about it. It's not nearly as important to the patient."

"But don't people want to know what they are up against?" the student asked in follow-up. He was one of those students who seemed to think he would get extra credit for challenging the professor.

"Absolutely. Patients like to know what's causing their discomfort or their disability. The fear of the unknown is always worse than fear attributed to something. In the end, though, it's more about the discomfort or the disability than the name or label."

She paused again for emphasis. "People care mostly about whether a disease will change the way they live. *Will I die from my disease? Will I be able to walk or care for myself? Will I be able to care for my husband, wife, or children? Will it hurt?* This is what patients care about most."

She was right, of course. When a car runs you over, you don't much care about the make or model.

"THERE ARE TIMES when I'm so ashamed at how I handled things," Joan said to me. "I just wish I had known more." She looked at her daughter for moral support.

"I think you have to learn it for yourself," Robin added. "There are times when I think we both failed my father."

"How so?" I asked.

"We just didn't know how to deal with him," Robin said. "Sometimes we'd get so frustrated and impatient with him. Other times, we'd just get angry over trivial things. For example, there was a point in his disease where he forgot how to put the key in the door."

"Or fasten his seat belt!" her mother interjected.

"Right! Every time we'd go for a drive, my father would ask me to show him how to buckle his seat belt and I would go over it with him in painstaking detail, like I was teaching a young child how to do it for the first time. But he never got it. I'd get so angry with him that he couldn't do it rather than just accepting the fact that you can't teach something to someone who is 'unlearning' everything. Ultimately, I had to figure this out for myself. Perhaps every caregiver does."

Now Robin was getting upset. As the memories returned, so did the guilt. They had tried so hard—done so much—but they still regretted how they'd dealt with some of the day-to-day issues. The guilt is as natural as the frustration. I can only imagine the anger and irritation of constantly confronting a college-educated man who can't figure out how to button his shirt or turn on the television. You *would* get angry.

"Why can't you do this anymore? A child could do it." The difference is that a child is learning. A patient with Alzheimer's is, as Robin said, "unlearning."

Like so many others in similar situations, Joan and Robin had fallen into the trap of remembering the person who *was* rather than the person who *is,* the person with the dementia. When this fact hits home, when they realize they're looking for someone who isn't there anymore, the caregiver feels guilty for having been irritated.

"If only I could have had more patience or been more

understanding with him!" family members say to me. "He wasn't doing it on purpose."

"So many people have trouble knowing exactly what to do," I said to the Scheers, trying to relieve some of the burden. "Every caregiver experiences the same thing, the guilt associated with getting angry. It's ultimately something you can't possibly control."

Robin nodded, but I doubted she heard anything I had said. Intellectually, people often know that there's nothing else they can do for a parent or spouse with dementia, but it doesn't make the guilt go away. She continued her story. "I think the worst thing is that even after he was in the nursing home, I had so much trouble getting into the frame of mind just to see him. I would go to see my father, the father who had raised me, and get nothing back in return. You don't get feedback. I mean, how do you talk to someone who doesn't respond?"

Once again, the question was rhetorical. Still, I tried to answer. "I guess you do the best you can," I said. "There's value in just being there, even if you don't get the feedback you're looking for."

Joan reached over into her bag and pulled out a piece of paper. "I used to refer to this when my husband was alive and I would get angry or frustrated. It's from *Saturday*, a novel by Ian McEwan. This is what going to the nursing home was like for me: 'It's like taking flowers to a graveside—the true business is with the past.'"

We talked for another thirty minutes, covering many aspects of Larry's illness. I felt almost guilty about transitioning the conversation to address the real reason for my visit. Thankfully, when Oscar's name came up the Scheer family didn't seem to mind. For the first time since we had begun talking, Joan even smiled.

"You know," Robin began, "we really thought Oscar had missed the boat with my father. He was in the final stages of dying and we still hadn't seen him once. Not one visit.

"We had heard about his exploits in the past from others and we were really confused. To pass the time, my mother and I went looking for him and found him in the opposite hallway sitting with another patient. He looked real anxious. I remember my mother addressed Oscar and told him he was not doing his job. A little while after we returned to my father's room, Oscar suddenly raced into the room as if the clock had just started to strike twelve."

"Like Cinderella racing out of the ball," Joan added.

"It was only later that we learned another patient was dying on the other side of the unit," Robin said. "Oscar stayed with the other patient until he was gone. Then he raced over!"

A look of awe had fallen over Robin's face. Across the table, Joan seemed to share in the amazement of what they had witnessed.

"Oscar allowed me to pick him up briefly and then jumped off my lap and went right over to Dad. A few hours later, my father died."

Robin started to laugh. "Funny thing is that an hour or so before my father died, a hospice nurse came in to do her assessment. When she was finished, she suggested that we take a break. 'Your father still has time,' she told us. Mom and I both looked at each other, but neither of us wanted to go. We figured we should take our cue from Oscar. It was a good thing, too, because he was right. Had Oscar not been there at the end, we might have listened to the nurse and missed being there when he died."

"It's not that we trusted the cat more than the nurse," Joan said. "Not, exactly. It was . . . well, there was just something about Oscar. He seemed so convinced of what he was doing. He was so clear in his intention and his dedication."

Robin summed it up: "This beautiful creature was sending us a sign. It would have been wrong to ignore it."

"A DOCTOR CAN GIVE you a label but it's not about that. There's nothing in the name. You want to know how to deal with the disease, what it's going to do to you."

Joan's words echoed in my mind as I drove home. I suppose after Robin's story I should have been thinking about Oscar and his sprint down the hallway, but what her mother said had struck a much louder chord. I thought about my own health and the difficulties I had finding a diagnosis for my arthritis. Initially, I was relieved when I finally learned the name of the disease that had so rapidly changed the way I led my life. At last I knew what I was up against. I could wage my personal war against a named adversary. It felt very much like a war. I was going to beat it—if I died trying.

But Joan was right. Ultimately, it ceases to be about the name of the disease; it's about the need to maintain a normal life, to be able to live life fully and in the moment despite the diagnosis. I thought about my own functional limitations ten years into arthritis and how they have forced me to make changes in my life. I could no longer play tennis, downhill ski, or play basketball like I used to. Nevertheless, I was still able to get out of bed every morning and do the things that kept me independent. I could still button my shirt and tie my shoes. Most importantly, I could still carry my children up and down the stairs—something I feared might not be the case the day my son was born. I knew that one day these very activities might not be possible, but I was thankful that I could do them today.

Today I can and that is enough.

I went home and said hello to my wife.

"How did it go?" she asked.

"Okay. Joan and her daughter are really nice people. It was tough for them, remembering it all. They both really loved Larry."

"Was Oscar there at the end?"

I chuckled. "You know, when I first heard about Oscar, I thought everyone was just plain crazy. But the more I listen to all of these stories, it seems he's there almost every single time. The families all seem appreciative."

"Maybe we should open up a cat medical school and put you doctors out of business once and for all."

I rolled my eyes and turned to leave the room. I knew she was teasing, but she had that look in her eyes. The wheels were definitely turning.

"Hey, where are you going?" she asked. "I want to hear more."

"Upstairs to take a shower."

She looked puzzled. It was only late afternoon.

"My joints hurt a little," I said. "The shower helps."

She shrugged.

I closed the bedroom door and got undressed. *Today*, I said to myself, *I take nothing for granted*. For the first time since perhaps my childhood, I thought about nothing else but the process of taking off each item of clothing. I undid the buttons on my shirt with a Zen-like deliberateness. I untied my shoes and took off my clothes, hanging them neatly in the closet. I turned off the autopilot and allowed myself to exist solely in the present. Nothing mattered but that very moment, and the next.

As the water streamed down from above, I felt the simple pleasure of it hitting my aching shoulders and back. It was warm and comforting and I was so very grateful for the simple pleasure of being able to bathe myself.

I was interrupted by a knock on the door. It was my wife.

"You okay, David?"

"Thanks, honey," I replied. "I'm fine."

Yes, it really is all about function and about learning to play the hand you're dealt.

CHAPTER SIXTEEN

"Which is more beautiful, feline movement or feline stillness?"

ELIZABETH HAMILTON

"DAVID, CAN YOU STOP BY? I DON'T LIKE THE WAY SAUL looks. I think he's becoming septic."

It was Mary, and she had reached me on my cell phone as I headed to the university for a research meeting with several colleagues. One of the many things I liked about Mary was that she did not overreact. If she said a patient looked bad, I changed whatever course I had set for myself and headed for Steere House, as I did that warm spring afternoon. The meeting would have to wait.

As I entered the unit I was greeted by a tall, well-dressed man who was standing near the nurse's station, deep in discussion with Mary. Even with his back toward me I knew that we had met before. I think it was his accent.

I rounded the desk and acknowledged the pair with a quick hello as I pulled Saul's chart off the rack with the urgency Mary's phone call had instilled. I rifled through the pages for his recent labs and kept one ear tuned to the conversation unfolding in front of me.

"Mary, my mother's going to be much better off in the hospital," the man said.

Now I remembered. I had met him in the hospital months ago when his mother, Iris Duncan, had been admitted with pneumonia. There had been nothing extraordinary about her admission, and she had rebounded rather quickly, but I had spent considerable time talking with her son about his mother's care and her declining condition.

He was full of questions, which was to be expected. His mother had a serious disease that was progressing and anyone would have been looking for answers. But the tenor of our conversations suggested to me that he had not yet come to grips with the terminal nature of his mother's condition. He seemed to be in a state of constant negotiation. "What if we try *this,* Doctor?" he would ask, invoking some medicine or procedure he had heard of or read about on the Web. When I had explained why one tactic wouldn't work, he had been quick to suggest another. Listening to him now, I could tell that nothing had changed.

"George," Mary was saying, "your mother's really not doing well. I think she's got another bout of pneumonia brewing and with the infection she's more confused than ever. Are you sure you want us to send her over to the hospital again? You know, we can treat her with antibiotics here in the nursing home where we all know her and she's comfortable with her surroundings."

The offer sounded reasonable and for a moment George seemed to waver from his initial insistence that his mother be rushed to the hospital. Maybe he could be persuaded that keeping his mother in the nursing home would be in her best interest.

He turned to me.

"It's Dr. Dosa, right?"

"How are you, George?" I was glad to have overheard Mary using his name.

"It's good to see you again. Will you be taking care of my mother when she goes to the hospital?"

I shook my head no. "One of my other colleagues is covering the hospital this week. But I do know your mother, George, and I agree with Mary that her dementia is getting worse. She's usually out here, sitting by the desk—and she's always been quick with her hellos in that delightful accent of hers. Lately, though, I haven't seen that same resilience. If you like, I can give your mother's doctor a call. I think treating her here would be in her best interest."

But his mind was made up. As George walked away, Mary turned to me.

"How do you know George?"

"We met a few months back when his mother was in the hospital. I think we talked for almost an hour on one occasion. He had so many questions about his mother's care. He literally wanted to know everything."

Mary laughed. "He's very involved. Even when he's traveling for his job, I get phone calls from him every day: 'How's my mother doing? Is she eating? Resting okay?'" She sighed. "Though, honestly, I hope that when it's my time, one of my kids will be as involved with my care as George is with his mother's."

"I tried to talk to him about hospice for his mother before," I said. "Did they ever get involved?"

"He's nowhere near ready for that, David."

But she may be, I thought. "What's her condition now?" I asked.

"Same as before. The X-ray says she's got pneumonia again, and she's confused."

"Has Oscar been by?"

Mary laughed. "Of all the patients on the floor, Oscar probably hides from her the most. She's always chasing him. Half the time, she tries to pull his tail. I'm not sure Oscar's going to want to be there when she goes."

"Is she still full code?" I wanted to know whether or not we would conduct CPR if her heart or breathing ceased.

"Uh-huh."

"I remember the first time I met her in the hospital," I said. "Even when she was ill, she was so vibrant!" Her smile could light up a room, but she had deteriorated since then.

"There are times when I still can't believe what this disease does to people," Mary said. Her thoughts must have been running on a similar track. "I think Iris has actually been at Steere House longer than I have. When she was first admitted to the dementia unit downstairs, people used to confuse her for one of the staff. She was such an educated, articulate woman. I think Columbia University actually gave her a college scholarship to come there from St. Kitts."

"So *that's* where the accent is from!"

"When I first met Iris, she was actually tutoring some of our aides downstairs on their English," Mary continued. "She was also an ordained minister, and I remember hearing her talk to at least one aide about her faith."

Mary smiled at the memory. "I always thought it was funny that she could still teach English and recite the Bible, chapter and verse, despite her condition. You never lose those teaching skills, I guess."

"But you called me about Saul," I reminded her.

"He may very well be the *second* hospital admission today," she said. "Go take a look at him and see what you think. You'll find Barbara there. She's very concerned." With that Mary turned toward her office, a copy of Iris Duncan's chart in her hands. As I left she was calling the medics to bring her to the hospital.

ONE LOOK AT SAUL and I understood Mary's concern. He was in bed rather than his recliner. The television was off and there was no life in his eyes; he seemed unable to keep them open for even a few seconds. His daughter was seated at the bedside, holding his hand.

"How's he doing?" I asked.

Barbara stood up and looked at me. I could see the worry in her face. "Not well, Doctor. Mary called me in to see him."

She stood aside to allow me to examine her father. I measured his blood pressure and confirmed that it was low. I felt his thready pulse and listened to his lungs. As I examined his legs, it was obvious where the infection was coming from. They were red and swollen. An area near his shin was openly weeping, a result of cellular fluid being pushed to the surface from damaged cells.

"He's pretty sick, Barbara. I think he may be septic, a condition where the bacteria in his leg have gotten into his blood."

She nodded but said nothing.

"You know, I don't think we can handle this degree of illness over here. We're going to have to make a decision about whether to hospitalize him."

"Whatever you think, Doctor." This did not sound like the woman who had always been so resistant to the idea of not treating her dad. I decided to use this opening to revisit his end-of-life wishes.

"Barbara, I know when your father was first admitted, you had requested that we do everything in our power to restart his heart if it stops. I'd like to talk about that if we could."

"Well, if you can save him, I think you should try."

"You know, it's not like it is on TV."

She gave me an odd look and I felt like I was in danger of crossing a line but persevered.

"On television, they always get everyone back," I said. "It's not like that in real life."

"I know that," she said rather coolly.

"In cases like your father's, where someone has a chronic medical illness like dementia, we're very rarely able to get someone back if their heart or breathing stops. On television, patients almost always survive. In reality, based on your father's age and his medical problems, I very much doubt we'd ever get him out of the intensive care unit."

"Why wouldn't we do everything in our power to save him?" Now there was heat in her voice.

"Sometimes, when patients are really ill, all we are doing is postponing the inevitable and inflicting more pain. Regardless of whether we fix his infection, he'll still have the dementia. We could always keep him here and make him comfortable."

Barbara looked at me with anger.

"Doctor, my father wanted everything done to keep him alive. Even if there's the smallest chance that he can recover, I think he would want that. I'm not going to change his wishes now."

I wasn't surprised by her response. I was a traveling salesman pitching an unpopular product: the reality check. I considered reminding her that her father's circumstances had changed, but I resisted the temptation. It wasn't going to change anything.

"Doctor, I don't want to talk about any of this right now. My father needs medical attention and we need to get him to the hospital immediately."

I left the room to start making preparations for Saul's transfer. As I sat at the desk staring off into space, thinking about all that had just transpired, a visitor appeared from out of nowhere. Walking along the length of the front desk, Oscar came toward me and sat down next to the telephone. His eyes fixed on me.

"Why don't you go talk to Barbara, Oscar? Maybe you can convince her."

He looked at me and for a second I imagined that he was considering my request—as if a cat would do what you wanted even if he could understand you. Instead he rolled on his belly in front of me in an invitation to scratch him. I reached over and paid my due diligence as he began to purr.

"You're really just a cat, aren't you?"

CHAPTER SEVENTEEN

"People who love cats have some of the biggest hearts around."

SUSAN EASTERLY

"THERE WAS A TIME WHEN I THOUGHT ABOUT WRITING a book about my experiences with my mother. I even had a name! I would call it *The Lady Upstairs Who Looks Like My Mother.*"

I was sitting in the parlor of Jack McCullough's house in East Providence where he was telling me about Oscar's first patient, his mother.

"I had to learn to love my mother as the person she had become," he told me. "She looked like the person I grew up with, but she was different."

At that he leaned back and smiled wistfully.

It had taken a while to get up the nerve to call Jack. Unlike the other people I had interviewed thus far, I didn't know him. But Jack's mother, Marion, was widely considered to be the first beneficiary of Oscar's many vigils. She passed away in November 2005, when Oscar was still just a kitten. Not only that, but a little more than a year later, Jack's aunt Barbara also died on the third floor with Oscar at her bedside. His was the first double-Oscar family that I knew of and I figured if anybody could lend some insight into why Oscar does what he does, Jack would be the man.

"Call him," Mary had ordered one day as I ruminated about whether to contact him.

It's an odd request to make, though, no matter how many times I'd done it already. "Hey, would you mind if I come over and talk to you about the cat who was with your mother when she died?"

But Mary was right. Jack had answered me with an emphatic *yes*.

"I'd love to talk to you about Oscar and what he meant to me," he said.

The house was quaint, practically historic: The furniture was antique and had likely been passed down from generation to generation. We sat across an old coffee table from each other in a pair of recently upholstered wing chairs. Everywhere there were reminders of Jack's mother Marion and her sister Barbara.

In one corner there was a photo of a grayish tabby cat, a pet from years ago, I imagined.

"Was your mother a cat person?"

Jack chuckled. "*That's* an understatement! My mother grew up on a farm in southern Massachusetts. From her early childhood, she was always collecting stray kittens, feeding them with baby bottles and droppers. Her family always used to tease her and call her 'Momma Kitty' growing up because of all the little cats that would follow her around the farm." Jack leaned over to pick up another gray tabby that had ambled into the parlor to assess the new arrival.

"Dr. Dosa, this is Bijou. I always used to say that Bijou was a reincarnation of Mittens, the cat we had growing up." He pointed to the picture of the tabby. The two were almost identical.

He put the cat down and it scurried out of the room with incredible speed. "My mother always had this uncanny attraction to cats," Jack said. "I suppose they felt safe with her. Even cats that would not come to anyone else would jump onto my mother's lap. When I first got Bijou, my mother already had significant dementia and she lived in the apartment above me. I'd come home and look everywhere for the cat, and then I'd go upstairs and find him sitting with her."

Jack excused himself to make a pot of coffee. He handed me a small photo album before he left.

"I put this together shortly before my mother died. I used to bring it to her and we'd leaf through it and look at the pictures together."

The album was beautiful and well constructed. Thick expensive paper, expertly bound—it was the sort of thing Jack might have crafted himself or bought at a specialty store, not the local five-and-dime. As I admired the album, I realized how important the project must have been to Jack, how it must have helped him explore the very essence of his mother's life story and perhaps, if such a thing is at all possible, to prepare for her death. The book was his lasting tribute to his mother, and a way to invoke the more pleasant memories from earlier in her life.

It's ironic that, while Alzheimer's and other dementias rob their victims of memory, they leave the family and loved ones with *only* memories. It can be difficult for adult children to recall the father who liked to take them fishing or the mother who pored over their homework with them. Personal mementoes such as the one Jack had assembled can help.

I leafed through the pictures. There were snapshots of Marion's journey from childhood to adult life, culminating with pictures taken at Steere House. As I turned the pages that held so much meaning for Jack I was struck by how composed Marion appeared in all of the photographs. Even in her later years, she was an attractive woman, well dressed in fashionable clothes, with beautiful hair and a glowing complexion.

I paused to study one of the photos. A young Marion was captured sitting off at a distance from the photographer, and she was looking at something just out of view. In her expression was contentment, perhaps a little mystery. Jack returned with the coffee and I put the photo album down on the table.

"That's beautiful," I said. "I'm curious: Did the album help stimulate your mother's memory at all?"

"Sometimes," Jack said, pouring the coffee and proffering cream, "although I think it was more important for me."

"How so?"

"Well, you forget so much about the person when they have dementia. You look at them and forget all the memories from before. They're still there in front of you and they remind you of that person from long ago, but they're not the same. You definitely have to learn to love the person they become."

He offered me a freshly baked muffin that I inhaled.

"I know you wanted to talk to me about Oscar the cat," Jack continued as I nodded with a full mouth, "but I really think you should know a little more about my mother."

"By all means," I said, taking a sip of the coffee.

"I used to say that I had to make an appointment to eat lunch with her." Jack smiled. "Even in retirement, Marion led a busy, full life—whether it was with aerobics, her church, or any of the other things she was involved with. She was a woman with a good heart. She found the greatest joy in the simplest things: taking me and the neighborhood kids for ice cream, or starting up the car to chase after a fire engine that had just passed by our house. I mean, how many parents actually do *that*?"

He paused for a moment of happy reflection and then added, "She was a great mother, but she didn't have it easy. My mother was a single parent."

"Really?" I said. I realized that there was a lot I didn't know about Jack or his mother. "Was she widowed or divorced?"

This is not a question I'd ask a single parent today, but single parents were something of a rarity in the fifties, and I wanted to know more about this glamorous, kindhearted woman who would go out chasing fire trucks with her kids.

"Neither," Jack replied. "In 1951 my mom met a man she fell in love with. It was accidental—and instantaneous. He was the one true love of her life. They were together for forty-nine years until his death a few years ago."

"I'm confused," I admitted.

"My father was married to someone else," Jack said. "My parents had to keep their relationship a secret. They had an affair that lasted for almost fifty years—though I prefer the word *relationship*. I was the product of that relationship."

Jack paused to gauge my reaction. He looked me over, studying my features for a hint of a reaction. In today's world, this might not seem so surprising. But 1950s Rhode Island was a different universe altogether and it was clear that Jack's upbringing had not been conventional.

"I used to say that I got to know my father from the reflection in the rearview mirror of his car. He would pick us up and we would just drive somewhere—sometimes he would take us for a bite to eat and other times we would go to another town or place where people wouldn't know us."

Jack paused for a moment to sip his coffee.

"Dr. Dosa, to understand my mother, you have to know that she woke up every day and got dressed impeccably just in case it was a day she could see my father. She never stopped looking over her shoulder for him and that behavior never stopped—even in the midst of her dementia."

I thought about the pictures I had seen: Marion with the carefully applied makeup and the beautiful outfits. Suddenly they made a different kind of sense.

"More than you want to know?" Jack asked.

"Not at all," I said. "Not at all."

The mysteries of the human heart are not confined to medicine.

"These days, when I think back about the early stages of my mother's disease, I realize how naïve I was," Jack said. "Maybe you just don't recognize the early stages when it's your own mother or father. You make excuses for the little things. On one occasion, in the early eighties, I had to drop off my car at the mechanic. We had agreed that my mother was supposed to pick me up. Obviously this was before everyone had cell phones. I remember sitting at the garage waiting for her for over an hour, but she never showed up. When I finally got home, I found that she had gone off on another errand. 'Was that today?' she asked me when I caught up with her. 'I guess I just plain forgot.' In retrospect, I can see that this was probably the beginning, but I just let it go."

Jack rattled off a series of mishaps, equally trivial if taken out of context. "I remember she started to lose her keys. When she couldn't find them, she'd blame me for hiding them. I would try to reason with her, asking what possible motivation I might have for hiding her keys. It didn't matter. Each time she lost them she was convinced I had hidden them."

Jack shook his head and smiled wryly. "One time she left them at the supermarket on the deli counter. On another occasion, she locked them in the car—with the car still running!"

He was actually laughing now, though I was quite sure that none of it was funny at the time.

"You know, Dr. Dosa, you make excuses. I would tell myself she was just tired. I would tell myself she was simply mad at me for suggesting that she sell the house she had lived in for so many years. Eventually, though, I couldn't bury my head in the sand anymore.

"For me, I suppose the straw that broke the camel's back occurred several years after her symptoms began. Now, subconsciously I must have known that my mother was having trouble with her memory because I started secretly placing my business cards in her purse when she wasn't looking. I don't know why I did it, but I guess I realized that she might need me one day and not know how to reach me."

Jack smiled at his deception.

"Sometimes she'd find the cards and ask me about them. I'd tell her that they were there just in case, and she'd get angry with me. She'd rip them into pieces in front of me or simply throw them out. Luckily, though, she didn't find them all. I was at my job one rainy day when I got a call from a mailman in another part of town. He asked me if I was Marion's son and told me to get over to the Eastside as quickly as I could. Not knowing what had happened, I was frantic. I raced out of my office and jumped in my car. I remember very little about the ride over, but I must have been going through worst-case scenarios in my mind."

How terrifying this must have been, a call from a stranger on a cold, rainy day. The need to drop everything and just leave, not knowing what you're going to find. Naturally he assumed the worst.

Jack glanced off and for a second I felt he might cry. Everyone else I had talked to had. But he composed himself and it occurred to me that maybe he was done with crying.

"When I found her I remember thinking that this was as bad as you can probably ever imagine. You never *ever* want to see your mother the way I saw mine that day. She was drenched to the bone and completely confused. It was clear that she had been crying and her mascara had all run down her face, making her look like some tragic clown. I asked her where her car was and she broke down in front of me . . . she had no idea. She was so completely lost!"

He paused in his telling. He was reliving every brutal second of that day as if it were yesterday. When he began again, his voice was low and halting.

"You want to know the funny thing? Even the car event didn't really bring the disease home for me. I knew my mother had a problem, but I hadn't put it all together. It didn't occur to me until a few weeks later when I was at a party. I was telling a friend about the incident and he casually asked me if my mother had Alzheimer's disease. It hit me like a ton of bricks."

Jack shook his head sheepishly.

"All of these events were happening, and I didn't realize that my mother had Alzheimer's until someone uninvolved casually mentioned it at a party! I was in denial."

As he uttered the *D* word, I couldn't help but think how many people were like Jack. We all make excuses rather than deal with what we don't want to see—even if it is right in front of our noses.

"Mom's just tired today."

"Dad's just got too much on his mind."

We minimize symptoms despite a preponderance of evidence. We acquit the victim and avoid the obvious. The mind really *does* work in mysterious ways.

"After my mother was diagnosed, I realized I needed to move her closer to me, so I relocated her to an apartment above my own. Thankfully, she let me take over her finances with minimal resistance and I eventually began taking her to the local senior center so I could go to work during the day. At first she complained bitterly, but I was persistent. I had no choice. But if there's a silver lining with Alzheimer's it's that they stop complaining as the disease gets worse. After a few weeks of resistance I think she actually enjoyed the senior center. Regardless, it only worked for a time. She became increasingly difficult for me to care for and I had to hire people to help, to make sure she got dressed in the morning, took her medications—and to make sure she didn't disappear out of the apartment while I was at work!

"Her personality also changed," Jack recalled. "She would swing from one extreme to the other almost minute to minute. My sweet, loving mother became paranoid and mean—something she *never* was earlier in life. I would be at work and receive a phone call from an aide who would be in tears over something my mother had done. I would run home and find this docile, sweet woman with no memory of having done anything untoward. Over time, the personality changes became extreme.

"Finally, the whole caregiver thing became exhausting. After all, they don't stop being ill to give you a break. Even though my partner understood, our relationship suffered. I didn't leave town for over four years. I became withdrawn and depressed. My blood pressure went up and I had a very hard time watching my mother disappear. I even started going to therapy to come to grips with everything. The therapy helped me understand that I needed help and that my mother needed to be in a nursing home."

"Did it make you feel guilty?" I asked.

"Initially, but I didn't feel guilty for long because it had to happen. In the end, though, once I got her into Steere House, I knew it was the right thing. We had a tough transition; my mother had been at another nursing home where things didn't work out.

"Ultimately, I was so happy to get my mother into Steere House. Aunt Barbara had also come down with dementia and was already living there. I was able to get my mother into the same room as her on the third floor. You know, my mother and Barbara lived together for sixty-eight years. They were apart for about ten years, but when they got back together at the nursing home, it was like they had never been apart."

Jack laughed. "The two of them loved their animals," he said. "I'm sure they thought that they owned those two cats. I'd come into the nursing home and find my mother in her room, but Barbara was always missing. I'd go hunting for her and find her sitting in some random room with one of the cats curled up in her lap. She'd light up and tell me that her kitty was here."

"What about your mother?"

"Oh, she was the same. There were times when I thought that my mother no longer recognized me, but she would always light up when one of the cats was in the room. Both of them. I would put one of the cats on their beds and they would just smile.

"The strangest thing is that my mother and aunt eventually forgot almost everything. They couldn't remember my name, where they were, or who they were. Yet those feelings—well, they remained. It was the same if there was a baby on the floor or if a certain tune was playing on the radio. Even in the end, they would simply light up."

"So, was Oscar there at the end?" I asked.

"The nurses tell me that Oscar was at Barbara's death. He came in a few hours beforehand and she died shortly thereafter. I wasn't there when my aunt died, but I can tell you what happened to my mother with Oscar."

Jack grinned.

"When Oscar was just a kitten, I used to bring him into my mother's room and put him on the bed. He would stay there for a minute or two, and then he would leave. You know what kittens are like."

Actually, I didn't.

"It was great for my mother, but he never stayed long. During the last week, when my mother was unconscious, Oscar would come into the room, look around or jump onto the bed for a moment, and then leave. On the night my mother died, the night nurse called me in to see my mother. She told me my mother wasn't doing well and that I should be there. When I got to the room, the lights were dim and they had started doing aroma therapy. I went to the bedside and was stunned to see Oscar lying there on the bed, curled up next to my mother. When I sat on the bed, he didn't budge; he just sat there purring."

Jack now wore a look of befuddled amazement.

"Seeing Oscar there at the bedside, I looked at my partner of eleven years, who was always there for me and my mother, and told him we were not leaving. As I said, my mother had this unique connection with cats and I knew this was the way she was going to die, with a cat at her side. Two hours later, my mother took her last breath. Oscar never moved until she died. Then he got up casually, like nothing had happened, and left the room."

We sat in silence. I was picturing Oscar. I bet Jack was too.

"I suppose my mother would have been happy to know that she died with one of the critters she loved the most. But to tell you the truth, all I felt was relief. I'd like to tell you that I felt horrible when my mother died, but I didn't. I think Ronald Reagan's daughter said it best for all of us when she called her memoir of her father's Alzheimer's *The Long Goodbye*. Every day I miss the mother I had sixteen years ago, but not the person she became. It was like watching a kid, but having them unlearn everything they knew."

I thought back on my conversation with the Scheers, who had voiced the same complaint. It must be like watching a film of a person's life run backward, I thought, except the person doesn't get any younger.

I asked Jack if he had any last thoughts about his experiences. He considered for a while before responding.

"You have to learn to love the person they become and find moments of happiness in the little things," he said. "That's why those animals at Steere House are so important. Dementia is all about comfort and distraction. I always felt okay about leaving my mother and Barbara because they had excellent care, each other, and they had their cats."

Standing at the doorway as I took my leave, I shook Jack's hand. Before I could go he offered one last thought.

"You know, Oscar the cat was not just a distraction for my mother," he said. "He was my distraction as well."

CHAPTER EIGHTEEN

"It always gives me a shiver when
I see a cat seeing what I can't see."

ELEANOR FARJEON

ONCE AGAIN, I HAD GONE OFF IN SEARCH OF ANSWERS and had come back with only more questions. Regardless, my visits were providing me with fresh insights into the disease that was afflicting so many of my patients and their family members. In a way, they were making me a more empathetic doctor.

I thought of Mary—my sounding board in this process, my confidante—and what made her so good at her job. I'm sure so much of her caring and compassion is innate; still, I also knew that she'd been through a lot.

This former beauty queen—she had been Miss Cranston, Rhode Island—had married the man of her dreams, only to find herself in an abusive relationship. When she reported him to the police, he killed himself in retaliation.

Having lived through that and singly raised two kids to college age, Mary was a tough customer who relentlessly focused on the positive. She was still full of surprises. Once, after she had pointed out the house where Talking Heads used to play, back in their days as students at the Rhode Island School of Design, she casually announced, "I used to go out with David Byrne."

As I said: full of surprises.

But the sight of her and the bleak expression on her face tempered any enthusiasm I felt and put my sense of wonder on ice.

"What's going on?" I asked when I found her frowning in her office.

"Nothing, David. It's just a bad day."

Mary stared off into space. I said nothing but didn't take my eyes off her. Eventually she opened up.

"Well, it turns out that the state of Rhode Island in its infinite wisdom isn't giving us the same amount of per-patient funding this year as they did last, and the administrator is threatening more cuts."

Every year, it's the same thing. The state asks us to do more and more with less and less. In a bleak economy, nursing homes are easy targets for bureaucrats looking to trim the budget anywhere they can. It's not like our patients line up outside of their legislator's office to protest.

Mary's news hit me like a wet blanket and I sat down in my chair with a thud. I knew that she was upset. Jobs were at stake and Mary was a perfectionist. She didn't like the idea of potentially compromising the care of her residents.

"So, who are you here to see?" Mary asked, attempting to put a smile back on her face.

"I wanted to check on Ruth. How's she doing?"

"Much better, actually. Her delirium has improved and she's eating again. I even saw her husband walking down the hallway with her earlier today. They were holding hands and it was really quite cute."

Mary's mood seemed to lift but the moment was short-lived. Her expression turned bleak again.

"Have you seen Saul?" she asked. It was almost a whisper.

"Not since shortly after he was admitted to the hospital," I said. He'd been over there for several weeks now, getting progressively worse.

"His daughter called today. She didn't sound so good. I guess he's in the intensive care unit now and not doing well."

The news wasn't surprising to me. Saul had been close to death when he left the home and I knew then it was just a matter of time. I looked off down the hallway in the direction of his old room.

"I wish . . ." I started but didn't finish my statement. Truthfully, I didn't know what I wished anymore. Saul had been pretty explicit about his wishes earlier in life—he wanted everything done, he kept saying. Yet his circumstances had definitely changed. Somewhere in the back of our minds, I know that most of us have a vision of how we would like to die. I was quite certain that Saul's vision didn't involve his current condition. But it didn't matter. The die had been cast.

"I know, you wish she'd have left him over here on hospice where Oscar could take care of him."

"I think it has less to do with the cat and more to do with the care that you and your staff provide up here. But yes, if I were in Saul's condition, I know I'd rather be here—cat or no cat!"

Invoking Oscar finally brought a smile to Mary's face. "Speaking of our friend, why don't you go take a look in Saul's room?"

I hesitated. I knew he wasn't there and I had come to see Ruth, and still felt that I hadn't been of much solace to Mary.

"Go on," she said.

I walked down the hall toward Saul's room. On the way I passed Ruth and Frank walking together, hand in hand. I said my hellos. Ruth greeted me with a warm smile.

"You're looking much better, Mrs. Rubenstein," I said. Though I sensed some recognition, I didn't expect her to respond, so I asked her husband, "Is she eating again?"

Frank smiled from ear to ear. "Like she's just come off a hunger strike!" With that, he vigorously shook my hand.

I may have actually smiled. I knew it was a temporary victory, but I was happy for them nonetheless.

I WASN'T QUITE SURE what I expected to see in Saul's room. It was dark and his belongings were laid out meticulously in preparation for his return. His bed had been carefully made; the comforter was drawn up above his pillow. Then I saw something move. In the dim light I recognized the shape of a cat. Oscar had started his vigil without the patient.

On my way over to the hospital, I thought about Barbara's decision to keep her father alive at all costs. Who was I to judge? It was so difficult to make that final call, to allow your parent or loved one to slip away. Maybe it was even a little unfair to burden a family member with such a terrible decision. Saul had insisted that he wanted everything done—back when he could still insist, back when he knew who he was. *To each his own,* I thought as I rode the elevators to the ICU, but I knew deep inside that I'd have chosen the cat.

There's little privacy in the intensive care unit. The doors to the rooms are almost always open wide so that nurses and staff can monitor their sick charges more effectively. These days the majority of ICU patients are older—in their eighties and beyond.

Room 19 was no different. A frail, graying man lay asleep in bed. A blue heating blanket covered much of his torso; it looked like a float that my son or daughter would use in a swimming pool. The blanket, filled with warm air, provided needed warmth to a body unable to fully generate its own heat. I barely recognized Saul. The nameplate on the chart confirmed his identity. Approaching his bed, I could see that a three-pronged intravenous line had been inserted into his neck. A dialysis machine was parked at the bedside. It was an ominous development for a man who never had any problems with his kidneys.

"I'm Dr. Dosa, Saul's primary care doctor," I said, introducing myself to the nurse who was standing in the corner charting at a computer. She acknowledged me with a brief nod before returning her attention to her notes.

"How's he doing?" I asked.

"Not good. He's still got low blood pressure on dobutamine and dopamine. His kidneys are failing, and the doctors are thinking about starting dialysis." The nurse shrugged. "We're doing everything we can."

I walked over and looked at the IV medications hanging from poles positioned above his head. He was on three antibiotics, all with expensive-sounding names: linezolid, Vancomycin, and ceftazidime. None of these medications had done anything thus far to threaten the bacteria in his bloodstream. The little buggers were winning and it was only a matter of time.

"The cardiologists are coming up here this afternoon to perform a transesophageal echocardiogram. They think his heart valves are seeded with bacteria," the nurse said, looking up from her computer.

I shook my head. Would he have wanted any of this? Certainly the trip to the hospital had been reasonable. But life events often get in the way of good intentions. Within a day, Saul's breathing had become labored, and his blood pressure bottomed out. Phone calls were made to the family. "He's hypotensive and we're going to need to put a tube in his lungs to help him breathe."

Looking at Saul, I realized he would now have a probe stuck down his esophagus in order to determine if his heart valves were also involved. Yet it wouldn't change anything even if the test proved positive. He certainly wasn't a candidate for surgery in his current state.

"Are you sure that all this makes sense?" I asked the nurse.

She shrugged. "Talk to the ICU doctors. Personally, I don't think so, but no one ever listens to me."

I smiled at her. "Me either."

My patient was way past autopilot now. No one would stop to ask if any of this made any sense. His breathing was labored, so they intubated him. His blood pressure was low, so they put him on medications. His kidneys were failing, so he was being considered for dialysis. Each treatment, procedure, and test made sense in the context of the latest information, but the big picture was absent. There was no consideration of the why; instead it was *full steam ahead!* I left Saul to his nurse's care and went in search of his intensive care doctors.

"Will it make a difference?" I asked the physician I found.

"Probably not. I think he's dying, but his family wants it done."

I returned to the front desk to call Saul's daughter. She answered immediately and I updated her about her father.

"The doctors here would like to put a tube down your father's throat to see if his heart valves are infected. Even if the test turns out to be positive, I'm not sure your father's poor condition will allow us to do anything to change his circumstances."

"Doctor, he wanted everything done."

"His circumstances have changed, though, Barbara."

"Everything, Doctor. Everything."

THE CALL CAME just after midnight. I got up to answer the phone, rubbing the sleep out of my eyes.

A young physician offered his condolences. "I'm sorry, but I just wanted to let you know that your patient Saul Strahan died earlier this evening. We tried CPR but we couldn't get him back. We did everything we could."

"Did you call the family?" I asked.

"We called his daughter. She took it really hard, but she's in with him now."

I told him to offer her my condolences and thanked him before hanging up the phone. I stared off into the darkness, thinking about Saul. I said a quick good-bye to him in the night air and then thought about his daughter. Did she get a chance to say good-bye? Probably not. I wondered if his minister had been by.

"What's wrong?" my wife asked, half asleep.

"My patient just died."

She muttered something unintelligible. In my business, these sorts of calls are not infrequent.

I settled back into bed, but found it difficult to fall back to sleep. In my mind, I pictured Oscar looking out of the window from Saul's room, perhaps gazing in the direction of the hospital across the street. I wondered if he knew. I am quite certain he would have been there, curled up next to Saul, had he stayed at the nursing home. In the end, all the procedures, tests, and treatments didn't make a difference. It was just his time. We all have choices about how we die, and some deaths seem better than others. I told myself that at least Saul was at peace. He'd moved on, whatever that might mean. I just wished the transition had been better.

CHAPTER NINETEEN

"Two things are aesthetically perfect in the world—the clock and the cat."

EMILE AUGUSTE CHARTIER

CATS MAY HAVE NINE LIVES, BUT WE ONLY HAVE ONE and we're all terrified to talk about the ending of it.

"Nobody likes to talk about death," Cyndy Viveiros said, looking at me across the desk. "It's like the dirty *D* word we aren't allowed to use in polite company."

I knew what she meant.

"During those last few weeks, very few . . ." She paused. "Look, I understand how hard it is for people to confront their fears, but for the most part, I was alone. Certainly the staff at the nursing home was great. I couldn't ask for more. But they would come and go at the end of their shifts."

She gathered her thoughts.

"Dr. Dosa, you asked me here to talk about Oscar. So here it is. I appreciated Oscar for what he did for my mother. But I also truly believe that he was there for *me*. During the last few weeks of her life, Oscar was in and out of her room all of the time, and I found that incredibly comforting."

"So, you think Oscar was there for you as much as your mother?" It reminded me of the last thing Jack McCullough had said to me.

"I think he was there for *me*," Cyndy repeated. "In fact, I'm sure of it."

"IT HAD BEEN a long three weeks at Steere House and I think I'd spent most of my visiting time seated in a chair by my mother's bed. The room had become my world. Unless I was singing church hymns to her, the constant drone of the oxygen machine and my mother's breathing were the soundtrack of those early mornings. For the last three weeks, the life had seemed to ebb out of her like an outgoing tide. There was a certainty to those days, though, a certainty that those were the last days of my mother's life and sometimes a certainty that those days would never end.

"The last day of her life, I remember watching the clock and rubbing my eyes. A lot. It could be two in the morning but I had no intention of leaving. Still, as the minute hand would trudge its way around the clock on Mom's nightstand I told myself that it would happen soon: one last breath, and then silence. At least that's what the hospice nurses told me to expect. Yet after days of watching Mom's chest moving rhythmically up and down, I wasn't sure that the end would ever come.

"Even Oscar seemed a little confused by her stamina. The cat that everyone said could predict death had been in and out of the room every day for the past few weeks, and nothing. But those last few days there seemed to be a greater sense of purpose to his stride.

"I remember that last day I was there he walked over to me and sat down. When I had leaned down to pet him he purred softly, so I picked him up and placed him on my lap. I rubbed that soft belly of his while we both watched Mom across the darkened room. Before long, though, Oscar had jumped off my lap and onto the covers. Then, look, I know this sounds strange, but he seemed to sniff the air, and then he rolled over on his back and gave this very catlike stretch. It was almost as if he was striking a pose," she said, chuckling.

Cyndy looked up at me to gauge my reaction.

"You know, Oscar can be very charming, when he wants to be!" she added, attempting to justify her earlier comment. "Well, at any rate, Oscar looked over at my mother and fixed his gaze on her. I wondered if this was his sign. I think I even asked him, 'Will it happen soon?'"

If he knew, Oscar wasn't telling.

"You know, Dr. Dosa, at first I had found Oscar's visits a little unsettling." Cyndy paused, unsure of what to say next. "I knew Oscar's game. I had even had dreams about him sitting on Mom's bed, terrible dreams that woke me up out of a sound sleep and always at the same time each night: 3:00 AM. It was just weird.

"During the first week of my watch Oscar would stroll by the doorway and stand at the threshold, peering into the room. At first I eyed him with anxiety, wondering if he'd cross over into our world. That's how I thought of that room, as my world."

Cyndy broke into a smile.

"After a while I came to realize that my fears were unfounded. I mean, for goodness sake. He wasn't anything supernatural. He didn't carry a scythe or a pitchfork. He was just an ordinary house cat. My mom loved cats. In fact, when

I had first looked at nursing homes, I thought Mom might take some solace from the animals running around the unit, and she had.

"Now that I knew Oscar, he wasn't threatening. In fact, he had offered me more companionship than anyone. I had a lot of concerned phone calls, and people tried to be kind, but in the end only two people actually came to visit Mom. I get it. Nobody wants to visit a nursing home, let alone the dying. It's like running into a burning building; the impulse is to run the other way. But Oscar, well, he was different. He didn't shy away. Actually, he seemed to know when he was needed most.

"You know, the first day I saw Oscar sitting in Mom's doorway I had watched him with a feeling of trepidation, I guess. He just sauntered in and walked over to Mom's bed. I knew what a visit from Oscar might mean, and I guess I held my breath. But instead of jumping onto Mom's bed he sat down beside *me.* He seated himself on his hind legs on the chair next to me and looked up at me, as if to ask how I'm doing. Can you imagine?

"When I reached down to pet his head, well, he gave me a long, loud purr as if he was real satisfied with himself."

As if, I thought.

"Then, just like that, he leaped onto the windowsill and settled himself in a classic sphinx pose. You know the one I mean, Dr. Dosa?"

"I do indeed," I replied. I really did know the pose. It was regal and mysterious, as if our own Oscar was descended from Egypt, as if he was in some way a temple guardian. Actually, maybe the idea wasn't too far off.

"Well, Oscar spent a good amount of time sitting on that windowsill, studying the world both inside and out. Each day he was there to greet me at the front door of the unit, and, well, he seemed to escort me down the hall to Mom's room. He'd stay with me for the whole visit.

"I really warmed to the little guy, you know? Soon I even found his presence comforting. When I felt anxious, which I often did, I would talk aloud to Oscar and he seemed to listen. He never passed judgment or offered unwanted advice, he just listened. When I needed a break from the room, Oscar would stay with Mom while I went out to stretch my legs or grab a bite to eat. Sometimes he would even escort me down the hallway toward the unit doors.

"You know, Dr. Dosa, I had a lot of time to think, sitting there with Mom, and I wondered how I would feel when she finally passed. I had experienced so much guilt during the long duration of Mom's illness that I had begun to think of guilt as my birthright, something passed down to me like a family heirloom. How had I not noticed my mother's illness sooner? Did I do a good enough job dividing my time and attention between my children, my full-time job, and my needy mother? Did I do the right thing by putting her into the nursing home when I did?

"No matter how much I did there always seemed so much more to do, so much always undone."

Cyndy paused for a minute, to laugh or cry, I wasn't sure. I don't think she was sure either.

"Now I realized that I was beginning to feel guilty for *not* feeling guilty. In truth, my mother's death seemed a natural end to her suffering. *But why do I feel okay with it?* I asked myself.

Searching for solace, I grabbed my mother's rosary from the bedside table and began to recite the Lord's Prayer aloud:

Our Father, who art in Heaven,
hallowed be Thy name.
Thy Kingdom come
thy Will be done,
on earth as it is in heaven.
Give us this day our daily bread
And forgive us our trespasses,
as we forgive those who trespass against us.
And lead us not into temptation,
but deliver us from evil.
Amen.

"When I was finished, I sat back down again, suddenly feeling very tired. For the first time I had a strong desire to go home. I spontaneously murmured a heartfelt prayer: *Please, Lord, just take her.*

"I closed my eyes for a moment and was consumed with a flood of loving memories of my mother from years gone by. They were comforting memories, and I allowed myself to almost drift off to sleep, listening to the white noise of the oxygen machine in the background. Suddenly I bolted upright. The noise from the oxygen machine was all I could hear. I looked over at Mom and realized she had stopped snoring. For the first time in days, she appeared peaceful. I looked at my watch. It was 3:00 AM."

• • •

"THE NURSE CAME IN a couple of minutes later and listened to my mother with her stethoscope, confirming what I already knew.

"She gave me her condolences and then left to telephone whoever was on call. For a while I just sat quietly in the chair watching my mother. Inside, I knew that she was gone but I still watched her, searching for movement. I leaned over and kissed my mother on the forehead, telling her that her beloved late husband was waiting for her. Almost immediately, I felt this incredible sense of closure, like both my mother and I were finally free."

Cyndy started to smile ever so slightly. "After some time passed, I got up and left the room to get a cup of coffee. I wasn't quite ready to call my family yet; I needed to wake up. I remember it being eerily quiet on the unit. As I'm walking down the hall, I hear this pitter-patter of paws hitting the linoleum floors next to me. I looked down and saw Oscar walking next to me."

I could picture Oscar walking alongside Cyndy, matching her gait, keeping pace.

"So, he was, like, your companion for those three long weeks?" I asked.

Cyndy nodded and I could see the awe dawning on her expression. I had seen this look a lot, of late, as people talked to me about Oscar.

"Doctor, I remember walking into the bathroom to splash some cold water over my face. When I left the bathroom, Oscar was right there waiting for me at the door. I stopped in the kitchen to pour myself a cup of coffee. Then I sat down at a table in the dining area to begin to plan out who I needed to call. Suddenly, there was a noise in the chair next to me. I looked over and there was Oscar sitting on his hindquarters, eyeing me. It was like he was checking up on me to make sure I would be okay."

She smiled widely now. "You know, throughout this process, people would come and go. But Oscar would stay. He was really there for me. In fact, he was the last 'person' I saw that morning as I left the unit. He just sat there on the nurse's desk staring at me as the doors closed behind me."

CHAPTER TWENTY

"I love cats because I enjoy my home;
and little by little,
they become its visible soul."

JEAN COCTEAU

IT WAS TIME TO STOP. I HAD NOW SPOKEN TO A HALF dozen people whose loved ones had died with Oscar by their side. I had plumbed their memories and emotions, and learned a lot more about what Alzheimer's does to families. But I was still surprised by how little I knew about Oscar.

I didn't feel frustrated, though. While I didn't feel enlightened necessarily, I did feel oddly elated. The image I was left with was that of Oscar walking Cyndy Viveiros down the hall and sitting with her in the darkened dining area—as he had sat with her mother in her final days. Maybe that's all he was: a companion, a sentient being who might accompany one person on their journey to the next world, or another through the grief of losing one they loved—a kind of underworld of its own. Wasn't that enough?

Did it matter if he had some extrasensory power of perception, if he could pick up on impending mortality before the best minds of medicine could? Maybe he was just a master of empathy. Maybe caring was his superpower.

I needed to talk to Mary.

"I've been thinking about what you said, that Oscar has forty-one family members and when one of them is in trouble, he goes and stays with them."

It was a little before three in the afternoon and Mary and I were sitting in her office. She had asked the staff to assemble at the nurse's desk at three, and I had arrived in time to get a few words in with her before the changing of the guard. The worries of our last encounter—the latest funding crisis, the Sisyphusean task of running the floor of this nursing home—seemed to have vanished, and she was looking calm and collected. She was also being quite modest.

"Oh, David, that's just my theory," she said. "What do I know? You have to remember, I'm a dyed-in-the-wool animal lover. It's not like I'm objective."

"Objectivity has its limits," I said. "Remember, I started out not believing in Oscar. To be honest, I thought you guys were all a little crazy."

"You know what the sign says," said Mary with a smile. "YOU DON'T HAVE TO BE CRAZY TO WORK HERE—BUT IT HELPS!"

"But now I think that Oscar has some purpose," I continued. "Maybe he's meant to help the residents—the family members, as you put it. But also *their* family; they may be the ones who suffer the most."

"Don't forget the staff," said Mary. She was fully engaged now, playing Watson to my Holmes. "You can't work up here and not become involved in the lives of your patients. We come to love these people, David. Their loss grieves us, too. In the end, we often become as close spiritually and emotionally to these patients as their own family members."

"Does it help to have seen so many die with Alzheimer's?" I asked. "Doesn't it make it any easier?"

She thought for a minute before answering. "It makes it easier to understand what's happening," she said finally, "but not why. Why would anyone be afflicted like this? Why would God allow this to happen?"

Though we seldom touched on the subject of religion, I took a chance and asked her, "Do you pray, Mary? I mean, have you asked God why?"

She smiled without directly answering the question. "I don't think He'd answer right away," she said.

No, I thought. *He'll take a message and get back to you.*

"As I've said before, the thing you have to remember about domesticated animals," Mary said, as if she'd been reading my mind, "is that people started to keep them because they had a purpose. They worked. If you were a dog, you were herding sheep or something. Any cat that wasn't doing some serious mouse hunting around the farm wasn't going to be there for long. They had to earn their keep."

"So you think that's Oscar's job," I said, "to take care of people?"

Mary shrugged. "Why not? Maybe he's just more highly evolved than the other cats. Maybe it's his way of paying the rent." She checked her watch and smiled at me. "We're all just guests here, you know."

At that, the door to the unit opened and a parade of evening staff shuffled through.

Mary got up from her chair. "I've got to get the troops together so we can run our list. Are you sticking around?"

I shrugged.

"Please do. There's one more patient I'd like you to see before you go. Our sign-out should just take a minute."

A few moments later Mary was standing with her back to the door, addressing the afternoon charge nurse and four aides about the day's events. This was her daily change-of-shift meeting, when she would advise the incoming staff on what to look out for and which residents might need special attention. I took my place by one of the aides and tried to be unobtrusive as I listened in on the conversation.

"Over on the west side," Mary said, "there are a few things going on. In 312, Mrs. Carey seems to be—"

As Mary continued with her report, I began to daydream. Farther down the hall a handful of residents sat watching TV. This time of day it was probably one of the soap operas they seemed to enjoy. All that drama and nothing ever seemed to change. Behind them, I noticed the silhouette of a cat perched on the windowsill staring intently at the world outside. It appeared that Oscar was off the clock and had found a favorable place to while away the day. It seemed like there would be no deaths on the third floor today.

Mary's voice brought me out of my reverie.

"Dr. Dosa, you might want to hear about Mr. Grant. He's the resident I want you to see."

I turned my attention back to the group and Mary continued her report. "Mr. Grant has a pressure sore developing again. We're changing the dressings twice a day and it looks fairly clean. Just make sure that we turn him often. He's completely bedbound now so we really need to be careful that the ulcer doesn't get worse."

To me she added, "I need to change the dressing before I leave. Why don't you take a look with me in case there is something else you'd like us to do?"

I nodded as Mary wrapped things up. "Finally, there's Ruth Rubenstein. She's really rebounded over the last few weeks. She's walking again and her weight is back up. As you know, her confusion is finally gone and physical therapy has been working with her. By the way, Frank just got here and he's requested some privacy. Please keep her roommate in the dining area, out of respect. I think today is their anniversary or something and he wants to be alone with her."

When Mary mentioned the request for privacy, a few of the aides exchanged knowing looks. Requests for privacy between patients and spouses are not uncommon; still, sometimes the people who work here can act like schoolkids. Mary cast a cold eye on the smirkers and order was restored.

As the group broke up I followed Mary back to her office. "Now, why is the idea of the Rubensteins wanting privacy so funny to them?" she asked. "They're a married couple. Just because she lives here doesn't mean that they don't have needs."

Mary raised her head. "You know, one of the other male residents has been spending a lot of time in the room with Ruth lately. The thing is, she doesn't seem to mind his attention."

"Frank won't be happy," I said in a hushed voice.

"I suppose we'll have to tell him eventually."

"Please make sure I'm on vacation when you do," I said. I'm not sure I was joking.

Mary shrugged. "I've got to get out of here, so let's take a look at that pressure ulcer."

We left her office and headed down the hall toward Mr. Grant's room. Suddenly there was a scream and Ruth Rubenstein charged out of her room. The look on her face was one of pure terror and she ran past us without stopping.

A moment later Frank followed her out. He stopped when he saw Mary and me.

"Dr. Dosa, I need to speak with you," he said breathlessly. His face was a study in anguish.

I directed him down the hall in the direction of their room while Mary went in search of Ruth. We entered her room and sat down next to each other on Ruth's bed. Frank looked at me through eyes heavy with tears.

"Dr. Dosa, I need to tell you what happened today, but I need you to understand a little bit more about us first."

"All right," I said.

"Ruth and I were married shortly after the war. I don't know if you are aware of this, but we met at a concentration camp." He looked at me to gauge my response.

"I didn't know that," I said.

"Dear God, I still remember it to this day. It was late October 1943. I had already been at the camp for a few months." Mr. Rubenstein paused for a moment and became lost in his memories. A minute passed before he began again. This time his voice was low and uneven.

"They say when you get older that you forget. It's not true. I remember the past more vividly every day. In some ways, I envy my wife—she doesn't remember any of this anymore but I live with the memories every day. At night I dream about it: the humiliation, the suffering . . ." Frank paused briefly and looked at the floor before continuing.

"I remember the first moment I saw Ruth like it was yesterday," he said. As he spoke his accent seemed to become more pronounced, the Eastern European inflections and inverted sentences bubbled up through time to the surface. "She must have just arrived at the camp. She was dressed in a brown dress, torn. Her overcoat . . . it was still new, but stained now from travel. This heavy suitcase through the mud she was pulling. I still remember her long dark hair: tangled and dirty but oh! it was beautiful. For some reason—maybe it was fate—our eyes met. Doctor, she had the most magnificent eyes I'd ever seen. Most important, there was no fear in her eyes. She was in this horrible new place but all she looked was determined: She was going to live!

"So like that I fell in love with her. I had to know her. I walked over and offered to carry her bag."

Frank looked over at me, the hint of a smile coming to his face.

"She turned me down, but never once did I stop thinking of her. It was weeks before we met again. This may sound crazy, given our surroundings, but, Doctor, it was the happiest day of my life. From that day we were inseparable. For nine months we were together. Then suddenly, we were sent to different camps. Before we were separated we agreed that if we survived we would look for each other after the war. We chose a place to meet—a church in my hometown. Neither of us knew whether the other person survived."

"Mr. Rubenstein," I interrupted, "I can't even imagine what you went through."

He put his hand up to stop me from talking.

"Dr. Dosa, it was sixty-three years ago today that we met in the courtyard." He paused to allow the news to sink in. "For the first time since that day, Ruth does not know who I am."

As he spoke his tears poured down his cheeks. I looked at him in silence, unsure of what, if anything, I should say.

"When we came to the United States, we didn't have a lot of money. All we had was each other. We couldn't speak the language. Ruth cleaned rooms at the hospital and I went to school during the day to learn English. At nights, we would walk around New York City, looking in the store windows. Then we would go back to our little apartment and lay down together. That we could afford!

"Things got better. My English became not so bad and I got a job as a laboratory assistant. Ruth took a job as a nanny for a rich New York couple. She loved that job and those kids. Maybe because we couldn't have kids ourselves."

Frank began to tear up again.

"I'm sorry," I said.

He acknowledged my response with a quick nod before continuing. "We never had it easy but we made do. Our lives got better. I went back to school and finished my Ph.D. For my first real job we came here to New England."

I looked at Frank for a clue as to where this was going. Perhaps he realized that he was rambling. He stopped himself and looked at me.

"Today, for our anniversary, I brought her a dozen red roses and a piece of her favorite pear tart from that excellent bakery downtown on Federal Hill."

I glanced over and saw the unopened pastry box on the bedside table along with the vase full of roses.

"I walked into her room and said, 'Happy anniversary,' like so many times before. I sat on the bed and bent over to give her a kiss on the forehead."

He paused. "In her eyes all I could see was terror. Dr. Dosa, I was a stranger to her. She just started screaming. . . ."

It was as if all the air had left the room.

"I didn't know what to do," he continued. "I tried to kiss her and she just kept screaming. I put my hand up to comfort her and she slapped me in the face. Then she got up and ran out of the room."

I could see the red mark on his left cheek. We settled into an uneasy silence. Finally Frank spoke.

"Doctor, I don't want my wife to live in fear like this."

I looked at Frank. He had stopped crying. His expression was fierce, as determined as hers must have been back in the camps. I understood now why he had wanted to tell me the story of his marriage.

"Will you help me, Doctor?"

Deep in my soul, I knew where he was coming from—and I knew where he was going. His heart was broken; there was nothing left. They had survived; they had come this far and now he was alone. I put myself in his shoes and for a moment, I thought of how easy it would be to break a cardinal medical oath and do what he was asking.

"No," I finally said. "I can't help you with that."

There was another awkward silence that I finally broke. "Mr. Rubenstein, your wife is terminally ill. Physically, she's been doing better lately, but when her time comes, we can put her on hospice and just make her comfortable."

"How long does she have?" he asked me.

"Mr. Rubenstein, only God knows that."

He allowed my answer to sink in. I wondered what he thought of God. Maybe God no longer existed for someone who had experienced so much horror. "Doctor, in my mind my wife died today."

He gathered his things from the bed. "Please just make whatever is left of her comfortable and don't let her suffer anymore."

"You have my word, Mr. Rubenstein."

Frank gave me a halfhearted smile and stood up. He crossed the room quickly and then went out into the hallway. I followed him as he passed his wife seated at the nurse's table at the front of the unit. He didn't give her a second glance and she did not see him. Maybe she was fixated on the black-and-white tabby cat that had left his perch at the window and had come to the front desk to inspect all of the commotion.

When he got to the front door I buzzed Mr. Rubenstein out of the unit with my ID card. As he left he turned quickly and grabbed my wrist. He looked me in the eye.

“Thank you for all of your help over the years,” he said. “I know I haven’t always . . .”

His speech trailed off and tears sprung to his eyes again. “Please just make her comfortable, Doctor.”

I nodded and he smiled grimly through his tears. Then he was gone.

CHAPTER TWENTY-ONE

"The smallest feline is a masterpiece."

LEONARDO DA VINCI

GEORGE DUNCAN LOOKED AT HIS MOTHER THROUGH tired eyes. Only a few hours before, he had been 300 miles away on the job in southern New Jersey; his work as a bankruptcy liquidator frequently took him away from home. His day had started uneventfully. Then at four o'clock he had received the call he had always dreaded.

"George, your mother is not well," Mary had told him. Usually he was the one to call *her*—so much so that when he saw the Steere House number on his cell phone he knew it wasn't good. "I think you'd better come up here as soon as you possibly can."

Instantly, he regretted having left his mother. He had spent almost every minute of the previous weekend's Thanksgiving holiday in her room. It was clear to him then that her health was in steep decline. But Monday had come calling, and with it his work responsibilities. His mother's chronic illness and frequent hospitalizations had already caused problems for him on the job. As he hung up the phone, he had felt the guilt ravage his mind and body.

"I'm sorry," he had told his surprised colleague. "It's my mother."

When he arrived at the nursing home shortly before midnight, George was pleased to see a family friend seated at the doorway, as if she were guarding it.

"I didn't let him in," she had told George, pointing to the black-and-white cat down the hall. "I didn't want him in here until you arrived."

For hours she had fended off Oscar's advances into the room. Eventually Oscar had grown frustrated and had walked away. But she knew he hadn't gone far.

George hugged her and then crossed the room to sit with his mother. She stirred briefly as if she recognized his arrival but then quickly returned to a peaceful slumber. He watched her breathing. It was rapid and rhythmical but did not have the violence that marked her many earlier episodes of aspiration pneumonia.

George took his mother's right hand from where it lay by her side. He grasped it vigorously with both of his hands and then cradled it softly to his chest. He began to cry again. He knew he was losing her.

He sat there like that for a while, unaware of the passage of time. Then came a knock on the door. A cleaning lady quietly entered the room and disappeared into the bathroom. She returned, carrying several bags of trash. George looked at her through his tears and she smiled warmly at him. He bowed his head.

Then George felt a hand on his shoulder. He looked up to find the cleaning lady's concerned eyes looking into his. She put her cleaning supplies on the floor and sat down next to him on the bed. George let go of his mother's hand.

"Don't cry," the cleaning lady said and handed him a tissue from a box on the bedside counter. "Remember, you will see your mother again. We have an earthly hope and you will see her again."

George stared at her in amazement. He wondered whether she attended the same Kingdom Hall he and his mother had.

"Do I know you?" he asked. The lady smiled warmly.

"Not really, but I know your mother. I have been working here for eight years. In the early days, when your mother was still able, she was my teacher. She was the one who taught me about the Bible."

George began to smile.

"My mother was a remarkable lady," he said.

The lady nodded and then stood up to continue her work.

"You'll be all right," she said firmly as she picked up her supplies and left the room.

No sooner had she departed than a night nurse walked in to check on George's mother. She watched Iris's breathing and looked at her watch, counting the respirations. Satisfied that her breathing was unlabored, she asked George if he needed anything. He said no, but she left the room and returned momentarily carrying a sandwich. Seeing the food, George realized that he hadn't eaten anything since lunchtime. He picked up the sandwich and eagerly began to eat.

As he chewed George heard the fast pitter-patter of padded feet on the floor. He looked down to see a black-and-white cat sitting on the floor in front of him. He was not surprised.

"Hello," George said to the cat. "Are you hungry?"

Oscar simply sat there and they settled into a strange silence, each looking at the other. George offered Oscar some of the meat from his sandwich. The cat sniffed at it disdainfully. He wasn't there for handouts. Oscar walked over to Iris's window and leaped onto the sill. There he settled into a crouched position and peered out into the dark night.

Polishing off his sandwich, George got up and turned on the CD player. He put one of his mother's albums on and selected her favorite song. As the song began to play, Iris briefly stirred. George crossed the room and knelt beside her. His mother's eyes opened and she looked deep into his.

"I love you," she said in a moment of stunning clarity.

Her last words spoken, she was silent again, drifting back into a peaceful sleep.

George spent a few more moments at his mother's bedside. When it was clear that she was no longer awake, he grabbed a blanket from the closet and returned to his seat. Within moments the music carried him away and he was fast asleep, dreaming of a place where his mother was with him, whole, in an unbroken and undamaged state.

GEORGE AWOKE WITH A START. He looked around, momentarily disoriented. Outside it was still dark. Glancing at his watch, he saw it was four in the morning. He had only been sleeping for two hours, yet he felt surprisingly refreshed. Regaining his bearings, George looked over at his mother's bed. She was breathing rapidly. As he stood to walk toward her bed, the activity roused Oscar from his perched position on the windowsill. The cat watched as he took his mother's hand and felt her pulse. It was frighteningly fast, crackling like an electrical current.

George rang the call bell and a nurse arrived immediately to reevaluate Iris. She left for only a moment before returning with a dose of liquid morphine. She placed the medicine inside Iris's mouth and then put her hand on George's shoulder in a gesture of reassurance. As the medicine began to take hold, Iris's breathing became more deliberate and her heart rate slowed from its staccato pace. He looked at his mother's face and studied her features as if to memorize them. He knew that she was leaving him and he began to cry.

A moment later Iris Duncan drew her last breath in this world.

"ABOUT AN HOUR after my mother died, an aide walked into the room," George said.

We were talking on the telephone late one evening a few months after his mother's last night at Steere House. We had tried to meet in person, but George had been called away to Florida for business.

"She told me that she was going to bathe my mother. I asked her why. 'My mother has died,'" I said.

"The aide looked at me and smiled. 'Your mother has died, but she should be clean,' she said."

Somewhere a thousand miles away, I could hear George choking up briefly as he considered the moment. "I have to admit that I was puzzled by her response. I asked her if it was normal to clean a dead body. She told me that she loved my mother and thought she should be clean."

"I suppose Steere House has many rituals at the end of life," I said. "For example, the nursing home always has their expired residents go out the same way they came in—through the front door. No one ever goes out the back service elevators."

"Yes," said George. "For me, though, of all the things Steere House did for my mother, this is what really took my breath away. A few hours later, the funeral director came for my mother. Oscar stayed for the whole time, watching over her. When the funeral director came, they placed my mother on the gurney and covered her with a white sheet.

"They wheeled my mother out of the room and down the hall toward the elevator. When we rounded the corner and started down the corridor toward the main elevators, I realized that almost every nurse, aide, and staff member in the building was lined up along the hallway like they were part of a procession for a dignitary. As we passed some of the nurses, I saw that they had tears in their eyes."

On the other end of the telephone, George began to cry freely.

"That took my breath away," he said, his voice wavering through the tears. "I realized then that they were like my family."

CHAPTER TWENTY-TWO

"You can't own a cat.
The best you can do is be partners."

SIR HARRY SWANSON

ALL WAS QUIET ON THE THIRD FLOOR. THE RESIDENTS were tucked safely in their rooms and the visitors had gone. The only sound was the gentle hum from the dimmed fluorescent lights. With no one to disturb him, Oscar slept peacefully, sprawled out in full glory on the nursing desk like a big, furry stuffed animal.

From a distance outside came the sound of an ambulance, bringing some untold emergency to the hospital next door. Oscar stirred as the siren grew louder. He lifted his head to investigate. The siren ceased as the ambulance reached its destination and Oscar stretched and yawned. The fluorescent hum returned.

Mary was working the late shift. She was busy doing what she did much of the day, scribbling notes in a chart, content to know that the residents were at rest. Oscar watched her work for a few minutes before announcing with a meow that he was awake and receiving visitors. Mary smiled and reached over to scratch him under his chin. Satisfied that he had been noticed, Oscar dismissed Mary and turned his attention to his hind paws, licking them in slow, deliberate circles.

"Well, are you coming?" Mary asked him, standing up. "It's ten o'clock, time to pass out our bedtime meds."

Oscar blinked but did not move. Was he considering her request? He was a cat, after all, and his hard-to-get attitude came naturally to him. After a moment, perhaps after Mary's request had been recognized and processed, he leaped onto the medicine cart, sat down, and looked back at her as if to say, *What's taking you?*

"Okay, Oscar, we'll start on the west side."

The squeaky rear wheel cut through the silence, but no one was awake to notice. It was just Mary and Oscar, who peered over the cart, surveying the hallway like the captain of a ship gazing out at a familiar but darkened sea.

The door to room 316 was open and Mary entered, pushing the cart. Louise Chambers was in her bed, snoring peacefully. Oscar was disinterested. Mary paused to look over her medication list and then opened a drawer. She pulled out an anti-seizure medication, popped the pill out of its wrapper, and filled a cup with water. She then leaned over and gently stroked her patient's hand to wake her. Louise started awake and Mary waited a few moments, allowing her time to get her bearings before helping her to a seated position. Louise swallowed the pill easily and almost immediately fell back to sleep.

Mary stopped for a moment and picked up the silver Tiffany frame on her bedside table. A man in uniform was standing next to a World War II fighter plane. He held his helmet to his thigh with one arm and smiled proudly into the camera. He was tall. Studying his facial features, Mary immediately noticed the familiarity of his tall frame, his wavy brown hair and prominent brown eyes, and his clean-shaven, oval-shaped face.

Mary chuckled and carefully replaced the picture frame.

"At least now I know why you like Dr. Dosa."

Without a further word to her co-pilot, Mary headed next door, and to the next room, and the next, checking each resident, dispensing medicine where needed. Through each visit Oscar remained on the medicine cart, seemingly uninterested in his surroundings. At last they arrived at the room of Ruth Rubenstein, who appeared to be fast asleep. Here Oscar sat up, tall in the prow of his ship. He looked around and sniffed the air.

Something was not right in room 315.

In one swift motion, Oscar leaped off the cart and onto the bed, carefully avoiding Ruth's slumbering body. He gazed at his patient and considered the situation. He did not ask for a second opinion but circled—once, twice—carefully preparing a place to curl up next to her. Oscar looked back at Mary, blinking once as if to dismiss her.

"Are you sticking around?"

Oscar put his head on his front paws and pulled his body close to Mrs. Rubenstein. Gently he nuzzled her arm.

Mary stopped what she was doing and approached the bed. She assessed the patient, who was resting comfortably. Medically, there was nothing to do there, so she sat down on the bed next to Oscar and considered the family situation. Ruth had received no visitors since Frank died of a heart attack a few months back. She had outlived her immediate family, she had

no children, and her lawyer was the closest thing she had to next of kin. There was no one left to call.

Mary reached over and lovingly stroked Ruth's hair. She looked over at the empty armchair across the room. A knit blanket was draped over the back; it had sat there unused for months. Mary was sad for a moment as she thought about how often she'd found Frank asleep there, long after every other visitor had left for the evening. Sometimes she would have to send him home. Grudgingly, he would collect his things, kiss his wife good night, and trudge off to his car only to return early the following morning. But Frank had never returned to the floor after the day of their last anniversary. He continued his daily phone calls but no longer visited. One day there was no call. A friend found Frank a few days later, lying peacefully in his bed.

Looking down at her patient, Mary perceived the faintest hint of a smile across Ruth's face. Maybe she was dreaming about her husband. Maybe she knew they would be together soon. Mary thought of the Rubensteins' half century–long relationship and Frank's stubborn dedication to his wife in the face of everything she had lost to dementia.

"God, Oscar," Mary said, "he really loved her. We should all be so lucky."

Mary leaned over and kissed Ruth's cheek while Oscar quietly purred. A few minutes passed as the two sat in quiet vigil. Then came a faint coughing from the room next door. Mary got up and said one last good-bye.

"Good luck, Ruth. I hope he's waiting for you somewhere."

She turned to face the black-and white-tabby cat.

"I don't suppose you're coming with me?"

His only response was a purr.

"No, I guess not. Well, I need to check up on the rest of our family."

Mary made a mental note to check back on Ruth when she was finished with her rounds. As she exited the room, she looked over at Oscar. The woman and cat locked eyes momentarily.

"Thank you, Oscar," she whispered, then dimmed the lights.

CHAPTER TWENTY-THREE

"A cat makes all the difference between coming home to an empty house and coming home."

UNKNOWN

ONE AFTERNOON A FEW DAYS AFTER RUTH'S DEATH, I was seated at the nurse's desk on the dementia unit, scribbling a note on one of my new patients, when I was interrupted by a commotion. Looking down the hallway, I noticed Maya chasing Oscar at full speed the way cats do when they are bored. Intrigued, I stood up and watched as they sped down the hallway past Louise Chambers, asleep in her chair. Then they were gone.

The scene of cat chasing cat in innocent play made me smile. As Mary said, this third floor really was their home. I looked past Louise in the direction of the departed cats. The afternoon sun had just started to make its impression, setting the walls aglow. Soon it would illuminate much of the hallway, then fade. It wasn't a lasting impression after all. I found myself thinking about Ruth Rubenstein; her death was still fresh in my mind. An hour earlier I had stopped by her room. I lingered there alone. I studied the unoccupied bed, neatly made, and the barren walls. Gone were the pictures of her youth, her husband, her past. The room was no longer hers, save for the faint reminder of her perfume. That too would disappear in time.

The main doors to the unit clicked open, interrupting my thoughts. I turned toward the door and saw Mimi, the admissions coordinator, escorting an elderly gentleman and two younger women onto the unit. They looked like sisters. They were on a tour of the facility and Mimi was in the midst of describing the unit.

"This is our advanced dementia unit. It is forty-one beds and staffed by nurses twenty-four hours a day . . ."

Suddenly the door closed behind the family with a thud, locking them in with the residents. I could sense their discomfort, even from a distance. They listened politely to Mimi as she carried on with her explanation, but I could well imagine what they were really thinking: *How in the hell do we put our mother in this place? The doors lock behind you! What did she do to deserve this?* I've seen this before: the deer-in-the-headlights look of a new family.

Mimi led the tour down the hall toward Ruth's room. She pointed out key locations on the unit—the kitchen area, the dining room, and the nurse's offices. As they passed Louise, asleep in her chair, one of the daughters stopped briefly to consider her.

I could almost hear the questions in her head as she studied Louise: *Is she clean? Is she happy? Do they take care of her?*

She was looking for reassurances that they were making the right decision, that they were in the right place.

I didn't envy them.

The lady moved over and studied the pictures on the corkboard next to Louise's door. For the first time since she arrived on the unit, she smiled. Then she disappeared down the hallway, chasing after the rest of her family.

I returned to the note I was writing. Something brushed against my feet. I looked down.

"Hello, Oscar."

He had finished his playtime with his sister cat and was looking up at me.

"I heard you were with Ruth when she died."

Much to my surprise, he sprang up onto the desk and sat down, staring at me as if to say hello.

Our eyes met and he started to purr.

"What's up, Oscar?" I asked, nervously reaching out my hand. "What's going on?" What if he *was* like Lassie, as I joked with Mary all those months ago, trying to say someone had fallen down the well? What if Oscar was trying to *tell* me something?

He considered my hand and then moved his face in toward it as if to say, *Scratch, stupid!*

I relaxed and began to scratch under his chin. I pulled him closer and he continued to purr more loudly. We sat together, sharing a moment, before we were interrupted.

"Hello, Dr. Dosa. I want to introduce you to the Carey family."

I looked up to see Mimi returning with the family. Oscar saw them too and began to take his leave. He leaped out of my grasp onto the floor before sprinting down the hallway.

"Cats," I said, by way of introduction, and leaned over to offer my hand.

Both daughters smiled.

"Do you have any questions about the unit?" I asked, trying to be helpful.

"Do you always have cats here?" one of the daughters asked incredulously.

"Absolutely. We have two cats on this floor and four more downstairs, along with a rabbit and several birds," Mimi answered.

"That's so nice," her sister responded. She was the one who had been studying Louise earlier. She turned to the father. "Dad, Mom really loved cats."

Past tense.

"You mean, your mother *loves* cats," I said.

She gave me an odd look, perhaps slightly embarrassed. I realized how many of the families I worked with spoke of their loved ones with dementia as if they were already gone.

"Actually," I said, letting the poor woman off the hook, "we've found that the presence of animals really helps residents in the latter stages of dementia. Your mother will know that they're here."

"Really?" the woman asked.

"Yes, I didn't really think so myself at first, but I've spent enough time up here to realize that the animals really do make a difference for the residents and the families."

The woman gave me a questioning glance that I immediately recognized. It was probably the same look I had given Mary the first time she had shared her musings about Oscar.

"I suppose there is just something about animals that still gets through." I paused for a second. "I'd like to think they have something to teach us, too."

The woman nodded and looked around, "So, what do you think, Dad?"

"I think this is the place." He attempted a smile—an effort, given the circumstances and turned to Mimi. "If it's still available and you're willing to take care of my Lucy, we'll take the bed."

Mimi nodded and escorted the family out of the unit, deep in conversation about the various forms and paperwork that would need to be filled out.

As they left, Mary appeared from down the opposite hallway, pushing a resident in a wheelchair. She parked the patient by the desk and then reached over to give the woman a hug.

The woman smiled and returned the embrace.

"What was that all about?" she asked me as she rounded the desk to sit down.

"Mimi was here with a family. It looks like we'll have a new resident in Ruth's bed."

"We always do, David. They never stay empty for long."

The afternoon sun had faded now, like words written in water. Halfway down the hall I saw Oscar appear out of one of the rooms where he had taken refuge from the visitors. He looked at both of us and paused for a moment. Then he turned and trotted purposefully down the hall in the opposite direction. When he came to the last room on the right he stopped and appeared to sniff the air. Then with a flicker of his tail, he disappeared into the room. I looked at Mary with the hint of a smile. Was Oscar trying to tell us something?

I was listening.

Afterword

MUCH LIKE THE FAMILY MEMBERS I VISITED IN THE course of my Oscar odyssey, I have come to be thankful for what Oscar does and what he has to teach us about the end of life. But the question that people keep asking me is "How does he do it?"

I think back to a phone call that I received shortly after my essay about Oscar appeared in the *New England Journal of Medicine*. The caller introduced himself as a World War II veteran from Florida. He told me that he had been a medic in Europe during the war and that his job was to evacuate injured soldiers from the battlefield.

"Doctor, by the end of the first few months of dragging people off the battlefield, I could tell whether the person was going to live or die," he said. "If they were going to die, there was a sweet aroma emanating from their bodies. I didn't smell it if they were going to live."

There is a plausible biological explanation for that "sweet smell of death." As cells die, carbohydrates are degraded into many different oxygenated compounds, including various types of ketones—chemical mixtures known for their fragrant aroma. Ketones are also found in abundance during episodes of untreated juvenile diabetes and doctors are taught early on in medical school to sniff the breaths of diabetics to determine if their sugar levels are high. Could it be that Oscar simply smells an elevated level of a chemical compound released prior to death? It is certainly clear that animals have a refined sense of smell that goes well beyond that of the ordinary human.

A 2006 study, published in a leading cancer journal, suggested that dogs could be trained to identify microscopic quantities of certain biochemicals excreted by cancer cells on the breaths of lung and breast cancer patients. Similar studies over the years have also identified melanoma-sniffing dogs and earthquake-predicting fish. Is it outlandish to suggest that Oscar, a cat residing on a floor where patients with end-stage dementia routinely die, has merely learned how to pick up on a specific smell emitted in the final hours of a patient's lifespan?

Perhaps, but I like to think of Oscar as more than a ketone early-warning system. Ever since I was a child, listening intently as my grandfather read bedtime stories from Rudyard Kipling's *Just So Stories,* I have imbued animals with human characteristics and frailties. It could simply be that we see ourselves in them—the best of ourselves, sometimes.

On a floor where the staff has gone to great lengths to make the dying experience tolerable for the residents and their families, I'd like to think Oscar embodies empathy and companionship. He is a critical cog in a well-oiled and dedicated health care team. As the physician, it is my job to prescribe the appropriate medications and provide guidance to the family; it is the nurse's job to provide the appropriate care; it is the minister's job to provide the necessary spiritual counselling for the patient and their family; and it is Oscar's job to provide the critical companionship during the final hours. He is clearly part of the team and as much a comfort to the families as he is to the patient, though in some cases he is the only family the patient has left.

I don't really pretend to know the nature of Oscar's special gift—I am not an animal behaviorist nor have I rigorously studied the why and how of his behavior. Whether he is motivated by a refined sense of smell, a special empathy, or something entirely different—your guess is as good as mine. But I believe we can all learn from his example.

Though my interviews with decedents' families were meant to provide me with more insight into what Oscar does, I found myself learning a great deal more about the diseases that had destroyed my patients' lives than I did about the cat. For all the mystery surrounding Oscar, there was little mystery about the devastating consequences of dementia.

Today, there are over five million people in the United States with Alzheimer's disease and hundreds of thousands more with other less common forms of dementia. Without new treatments, estimates suggest that this number is likely to skyrocket as our population continues to age. But the tragedy of dementia is not measured merely by the number of patients directly affected. For every patient with dementia, there are many more caregivers whose lives will never be the same.

Recently, my wife and I joined their ranks when her mother was diagnosed with dementia. Like countless others in this country and around the world, we are entering an uncertain phase in our lives, one that will involve caring for a parent with dementia. We add this new responsibility to the myriad others of parent, professional, and spouse. Where will the extra energy come from?, we wonder. How can we find the capacity to care for yet another dependent—an adult, no less? Even though I work closely with caregivers who tackle the same issues, and have always respected their fortitude and optimism, it is always different when it happens to you and your own family. Suddenly it's personal.

After another exasperating phone call with her mother's doctors, who had nothing new to suggest in regard to her failing memory, my wife turned to me for support. "Surely from all of those interviews you gleaned some words of wisdom that might help me get through this?" While every case is different and all caregivers find their own way through trial and error, coming up with solutions as different as one family is from the next, I feel confident in making a few generalizations:

1. Take care of yourself.

As a geriatrician I have seen countless caregivers fail physically or mentally long before the patient with dementia does. There's good reason for this. Caregiving is a 24-hour, 7-day-a-week, 365-day-a-year responsibility. There is no time off for good behavior and the physical demands of caring for the elderly when they have dementia are profound. So too is the psychic strain of seeing someone close to you struggle. Remember, *no one is ever successful for long if they go it alone.* You need to share the burden of caregiving, even if it ultimately involves placing a parent or spouse in an assisted living or nursing home. You also need to maintain the body and mind by seeking the medical and emotional support needed to deal with caregiver challenges. The Alzheimer's Association has many fantastic resources; I've found their local support groups to be particularly helpful.

2. Be present.

Easier said than done—try putting aside daily work and life responsibilities and making the time to spend with someone at the end of life. Yet so many of our day-to-day responsibilities are ultimately inconsequential. Someone can always cover for you at work, and your children will forgive you for missing a soccer practice. Animals like Oscar can teach us through their steadfastness, their patience, and their presence. They don't have to be anywhere else except where they are. When Oscar visits his patients, he doesn't care what time it is or whether there is somewhere else he would rather be. He is in the moment. It is so important to be able to spend time with someone with dementia—even if you think that they no longer know who you are.

3. Celebrate the little victories but see the big picture.

Living with someone with dementia can be a roller-coaster ride. For every little victory that brings joy—an upswing in appetite, a remembrance of a name—there is the ultimate certainty of continued decline. Those that cope best with terminal progressive illnesses such as dementia are people who can gain satisfaction from a little victory without losing the larger perspective.

4. Become an advocate for high-quality care.

Our medical system does not effectively deal with patients with dementia. Certainly some institutions do it better than others, but ultimately every acute-care hospital, nursing home, and outpatient office could be improved. Being an advocate for high-quality care is about being involved and asking questions. It is also about choosing your battles and understanding the limitations inherent in dementia care, particularly in the nursing home environment. It is possible to get good care or bad care at every nursing home. What makes the difference is family involvement.

5. Love and let go.

It is my hope that, one day, dementia will become a footnote in medical history, much like smallpox and the plague are today. We will certainly be better at handling it. The treatment options available today, though, are few, and even those are seldom helpful for long. Eventually, every caregiver has to *let go*—whether it's letting go and sending a loved one to a nursing home or letting go when death is near. When this time comes, please remember that letting go of a person with terminal dementia is not a sign of defeat: It is an act of love.

Acknowledgments

I HAVE BEEN TRULY BLESSED IN MY LIFE TO FIND MYSELF surrounded by patients, colleagues, friends, and family who I learn from every day. A full list of acknowledgments would be simply too long to print, but I would specifically like to thank the following individuals for their assistance during this project:

First, I'd like to offer a special thank you to Sean Elder for believing in the project and helping me pull out what was good in the manuscript and make it better. I couldn't have done it without you.

I'd also like to offer my profound gratitude to the family members of Oscar's third-floor patients, past and present, who spent signficant time with me throughout the writing of this book. Some of you allowed me to use your names and stories in the book, while others provided background but asked for privacy. I can't possibly tell you how much I am indebted to the fact that you entrusted me with your innermost thoughts and personal demons. I apologize to all of you for any unintentional mistakes I have made in the presentation of the facts, for any liberties I have taken in telling your stories, and for any additional sorrow that I may have caused as we sifted through the memories.

Thank you also to Mary Miranda, who helped me collect many of the stories that appear in this book. Mary, it is through your eyes that I first saw how much good there was in Oscar, and the wonder in your eyes as you discussed each story was truly infectious. A special thanks also to the rest of the staff at Steere House and Home and Hospice of Rhode Island. Though your work is often underappreciated, I hope this book does something to correct this travesty. You are all the true Heroes of long-term care and perform your duties with more passion, love, and attention to detail than countless other professionals—including us doctors, who receive more praise and financial reward.

Special thanks also to Dr. Joan Teno for our many discussions about end-of-life care, the meaning of Oscar the cat, and your thoughts at every stage of the writing process. Please know that your mentorship, passion, and belief in the importance of end-of-life care have been profoundly inspirational to me. Thank you for being my sounding board over the years and, most importantly, a dear personal friend.

Thanks also to my other medical colleagues at Steere House, at Brown University's Center for Gerontology, the Providence Veterans Affairs Medical Center, and within the division of geriatrics. I have been fortunate to work with so many talented individuals over the years.

As any writer will tell you, there are hundreds of talented people behind the scenes who make each book come to life.

To Brenda Copeland, thank you for being my "cat guru"—

not to mention a fabulous editor. Thank you for taking the leap of faith that a first-time author with a good story could pull this off. You were always so complimentary and knew exactly how to take a newbie under your wing. From here on out until the day I die, I will always remember to "jump right into the story" and I will never—ever—forget to use contractions! Thank you also to Ellen Archer, Will Balliett, and the rest of the staff at Hyperion for your valuable insights into the manuscript and for coaching me through the process at each step of the way.

To my agent, Emma Sweeney, and her colleagues Eva Talmadge and Justine Wenger—you're a first-class organization. Thank you for keeping me on the straight and narrow as I've learned to navigate these uncharted waters. You've always steered me in the right direction. As they say in the movies, "I hope this is the beginning of a beautiful friendship."

In closing, I'd like to offer a heartfelt thanks to my family. To my "grandparents" Eva and Jan Rocek—thank you for your love, wisdom, and all of your life stories. I will always treasure those summers together at the lake house—even if I had to stay out of Puma's way. To Mellissa, thank you for being such an important part of our family. To my brother, Peter, and my parents Noemi and Stefan—thank you for your love and unconditional support through the good times and the bad. You are my role models in life, and I couldn't be luckier. Finally—and most importantly—to my children, Ethan and Emma, and my loving and supportive wife, Dionne. You are my reason for living and you inspire me daily. In sickness and in health, for better or worse, please know that I will love you always. And by the way, at the end of my days, I prefer the cat over the ICU.

A Conversation with Dr. David Dosa

Q: Tell me about Oscar the cat.

Oscar is a black-and-white tabby cat who lives at Steere House Nursing and Rehabilitation Center in Providence, Rhode Island. Since his arrival in 2005, Oscar has lived among the residents of Steere House's third floor dementia unit. Though outwardly he's "just a cat," Oscar has developed a unique ability to sense when patients on the third floor are about to die, and he holds bedside vigils for patients during their last hours.

In 2007, I wrote an essay about Oscar for the *New England Journal of Medicine.* His story drew international attention, but Oscar remains unfazed by this interest. He continues his "work" at Steere House, comforting patients and their families.

Q: Is there a scientific explanation for Oscar's behavior?

It's possible that Oscar perceives a pheromone or another smell emitted by a dying patient. Dying cells release sweet-smelling ketones and other cellular by-products that may be appreciated by an animal with a keen sense of smell.

Additionally, animal behavior experts have speculated that Oscar's talent is behavioral—that he's imitating the nurses and staff at Steere House. Perhaps Oscar understands when he is needed and simply wishes to be part of the team that delivers compassionate end-of-life care to the dying.

Q: I hear you were initially hesitant to believe in Oscar's ability. What changed your mind?

I'd like to be able to say that I was the first person to pick up on Oscar's unique abilities, but initially I was very skeptical. I suppose my ego balked at the notion that a cat could have a better sense of knowing when my patient might die than I do.

I became convinced of Oscar's abilities, though, when there were two patients on the floor dying simultaneously. All of the staff thought that one of the patients was closer to death, but Oscar remained attached to the other patient. At one point, a nurse's aide became concerned that Oscar's streak of predicting death would end, and brought the angry cat to the bedside of the more seriously ill patient. Oscar looked at everyone like they were crazy and sprinted out of the room, returning to his vigil at the bedside of the first patient. Oscar's charge died a few hours later, but the other patient rallied for a couple more days. Four hours before the second patient died, Oscar came to his bedside.

Q: How did Oscar end up at Steere House?

Steere House's animal companion program began years ago when a stray cat walked through the front doors of the nursing home and refused to leave. Eventually the staff named him Henry after Steere House's founder. Over time, members of the staff realized how beneficial animals like Henry were to the overall mission of making Steere House "more like a home than a nursing home." When Henry died years later, Oscar was one of six cats brought in from a nearby shelter to live at Steere House. Today, the animal companion program is an important part of the nursing home's culture change movement.

Q: Have any of the families of Steere House residents ever reacted poorly to Oscar's presence?

Thankfully, the response to Oscar has been overwhelmingly positive. Given the degree of memory impairment among patients on Oscar's floor, the patients do not attach specific meaning to Oscar's visits.

Only one or two families have asked to keep Oscar away during a loved one's death. On one such occasion, Oscar became distraught at having the door to one of his patients closed as that person was dying. Oscar paced backward and forward for hours in front of the room. Eventually, he even went next door, where he tried to scratch his way through the common wall to the room. Finally, the staff at the nursing home had to remove him from the floor.

Q: Five million Americans are afflicted with dementia currently. What is it?

Dementia is not a specific disease but rather a word used to describe a spectrum of diseases that affect the brain, causing problems with memory, thinking, language, judgment, and personality. Dementia may be static (e.g., the result of a serious stroke) or progressive. The most common form of progressive dementia is Alzheimer's disease, but there are several other categorizations as well. Although dementia is more common in the elderly, disorders of memory should never be considered normal. They should always be examined by a doctor who specializes in these diseases.

Q: What is the "Sandwich Generation"?

The "Sandwich Generation" is a term that describes the generation of people trapped between caring for their own kids and their ailing family members—statistics suggest that one in eight Americans is currently part of the Sandwich Generation. These numbers are only expected to increase as the number of senior citizens increases during the next twenty years. Recently, my wife and I have become part of the Sandwich Generation as we care for my wife's ailing mother.

Members of the Sandwich Generation struggle to balance the needs of each generation they care for and their own needs. Will I take my mom to the doctor or attend my daughter's ballet recital? Can I maintain my work responsibilities while tending to my parent's need for daily care? There is a tremendous amount of guilt that is wrapped up in making such decisions and the risks of depression, medical illness, and maladaptive coping skills, such as alcohol and substance abuse, are higher in this double-duty population.

Q: How is the care of the elderly changing in this country?

Right now, we are at the precipice of a major health care dilemma. Simply put, we are grappling with how to care for the "silver tsunami"—the enormous number of baby boomers about to reach their "senior" years. As our nation ages, the number of people who require complicated chronic disease management will undoubtedly increase as well. Unfortunately our health care system is ill-suited to provide optimal care to these patients. For example, there are currently fewer than ten thousand formally trained geriatricians in this country. Until we redesign our health care system to emphasize and reimburse coordination of care rather than specialty care, we will continue to have trouble meeting the needs of the elderly during the impending demographic crisis.

Q: How will the outcome of the current health care debate impact end-of-life care?

Our current system of health care is unsustainable—crucial funds need to be allotted for promoting end-of-life discussions with patients. As it stands, our health care system compensates doctors for "doing rather than not doing." We receive little to no payment for taking the time to talk to patients about their health care choices. It is not just money that keeps these discussions from happening. Doctors often fear litigation for not taking actions to save an elderly patient, and many feel like they are failing their patients when they speak of end-of-life care. As such, patients at the end of life often receive costly, unnecessary procedures and testing as a default. It's simply easier to do than to not do. For example, the use of feeding tubes has never been shown to improve survival or quality of life for dementia patients. Yet they are routinely inserted in patients with advanced dementia. One key reason is that generous Medicare dollars help to compensate doctors and hospitals for performing these procedures but not for conducting end-of-life discussions. Without health care reform that promotes these crucial discussions, unnecessary and costly procedures will continue without rendering any improvement in quantity or quality of life.

Q: How will the outcome of the current health care debate impact nursing homes?

The current bill before Congress may have devastating effects on nursing homes around the country. Nursing homes currently operate on the razor's edge of profitability. A delicate balance of government dollars, through Medicare and Medicaid, helps care facilities get by, but proposed Medicare reforms will take away crucial dollars from nursing homes, crippling our nation's long-term care industry.

A second threat is the reduction of payments to hospice organizations that provide crucial care to nursing home residents. Though such care has been shown to reduce costly end-of-life hospitalizations and increase family satisfaction with care, there is concern that the current health care bill may limit payment to hospice organizations.

Q: How do animals affect patients in late stages of dementia?

In late stages of dementia, patients are unable to care for themselves. Frequently, they have lost the ability to walk and to communicate verbally. For close family members, the biggest tragedy is often when the patient is unable to recognize them. Nevertheless, though an advanced dementia patient might lose the ability to communicate verbally, there are certain innate stimuli, such as music, babies, and animals like Oscar, that still seem to resonate with them. Even for those with the severest forms of dementia, the presence of animals reduces agitation and symptoms of depression.

Q: Have you learned about other pets or animals that seem to have a sixth sense about comforting the dying?

Although Oscar is unique, he is certainly not alone in what he does. Since Oscar's story made international news, I've heard from hundreds of pet owners about their special animals, including other health care facilities that have their own "Oscar." These e-mails and letters have made me appreciate just how important animals are to people as companions. They truly do seem to have a sixth sense about knowing when we need them the most.

Q: You live with the daily pain of arthritis. How has this chronic condition affected your work?

At the age of twenty-seven, I developed my own chronic illness, psoriatic arthritis, which has changed the way I live my life. I can no longer do many of the active things I loved to do in the past, such as play basketball and soccer. I wake up every day and have difficulty just getting out of bed. Yet strangely, there have been many profound positives to my disease as well. My illness has undoubtedly made me a better doctor, helping me become more empathetic. I find I am more aware of what it's like to be on the other side of the stethoscope, particularly the inherent fear patients have of "not knowing" how a chronic disease will affect them long term.

In fact, my battle with arthritis also brought me to the field of geriatrics and nursing home care. Shortly after I was diagnosed, I did a rotation in geriatrics and worked in a nursing home for the first time. Driving home one evening, I realized that I might one day end up a patient in a nursing home like the one I had been to that day. And I didn't like what I saw. I made a deal with myself that I would do my part to improve on the world I had seen that day, so that perhaps it will be different if I ever find myself admitted to a nursing home down the road.

Discussion Points for *Making Rounds with Oscar*

1. Dr. Dosa's patients' families frequently remark that their decisions about their loved ones' care (putting their parent or spouse in Steere House or opting for end-of-life care) caused them extreme anxiety. Think about the families of Dr. Dosa's patients. Do you think they made morally correct decisions about their loved ones' care?

2. In Chapter 3, Dr. Dosa discusses his fears about "ending up like Ida." Do you think his fears are rational or irrational? In what ways does discussing Oscar with his patients' families make him more empathetic?

3. Kathy Sanders, the daughter of one of his dementia patients, tells Dr. Dosa that the little victories and experiences are all that matter. What do you think of Kathy's coping mechanism? How is it different from the way other families Dr. Dosa comes in contact with cope with their loved ones' conditions?

4. In the book, Dr. Dosa discusses the difficulties of talking with patients about end-of-life care—particularly in slowly progressive diseases like dementia. Was Dr. Dosa wrong to suggest that Frank Rubenstein consider pulling the plug on his wife, Ruth? Why is end-of-life care so difficult to discuss in cases like Ruth's?

5. Barbara Strahan, the daughter of a dementia patient, yells at the nurses for losing her father's slippers. Was her reaction warranted? Why do you think she became so angry? In what ways does the staff at Steere House take the brunt of families' anger and frustration?

6. In Chapter 11, we learn that Lino Ferretti's wife often played music in his room, and that the music calmed him even when he no longer knew his wife. Why do you think music can comfort patients even after communication skills have been lost? Why do you think that animals at Steere House provide the same comfort? What are the similarities between music and animals?

7. Cyndy Viveiros refers to death as the "dirty D word." In what ways do you think our culture is afraid of death? Do you think our fear of death affects our medical decisions? How does fear of death affect the families that Dr. Dosa meets in the book?

8. Frank Rubenstein remains fervently attached to his wife, Ruth, serving as her staunch advocate. Yet when she forgets who he is, he leaves Steere House forever and asks Dr. Dosa to make her comfortable and let her die. Why do you think, for Frank, that Ruth's memory loss is equivalent to her death? Do you think Frank's absence is an act of abandonment or love? Why do you think Frank finally tells Dr. Dosa the story of his and Ruth's life together at that moment?

9. Steere House believes that all patients should leave the hospital as they entered it—through the front door. In our culture that shies away from death, why do you think Steere House adopted this policy? What purpose does it serve for the other patients? What purpose does it serve for the staff?

10. What do you think of Oscar's unique abilities? After reading the stories of the families he comforted, do you believe that he knows when death is approaching? Do you think he is unique, or is it possible that other animals are equally intuitive?

Al Weems

DR. DAVID DOSA is a geriatrician and assistant professor of medicine at the Warren Alpert Medical School of Brown University. An essay he wrote for the *New England Journal of Medicine* was the basis for this book. Dr. Dosa lives with his family in Barrington, Rhode Island.